THE GUITAR STYLE OF
George Benson

By Dave Rubin

CONTENTS

Cover photo by Neil Zlozower

ISBN 978-0-634-01132-0

HAL•LEONARD®
CORPORATION

7777 W. BLUEMOUND RD. P.O. BOX 13819 MILWAUKEE, WI 53213

Visit Hal Leonard Online at
www.halleonard.com

Introduction

The development of jazz guitar has been marked by a string of technical and stylistic innovators. In the post World War I era there appeared the revolutionary solo voice of Lonnie Johnson, one of the largely unheralded guitar heroes of the twentieth century who would go on to further achievement in the blues. His one time recording buddy, Eddie Lang, performing under the pseudonym Blind Willie Dunn, advanced the cause of chordal accompaniment as well as single-string soloing and is credited with bringing the guitar forward as a legitimate musical instrument. Following in the twenties are the notable soloing and chord melody accomplishments of George Van Eps, Dick McDonough, Carl Kress, and Nick Lucas. The thirties produced the wild gypsy genius, Django Reinhardt, a virtuoso whose fleet flights of fancy, octaves, and aggressive chording would also have far reaching influence.

The advent of the first commercially viable amplified guitar in 1936 by Gibson led the way for another genius and the acknowledged forefather of modern jazz guitar, Charlie Christian. Quickly realizing the expanded soloing potential of the electric guitar, Christian sprung extremely sophisticated, hornlike lines on his stunned contemporaries while in the Benny Goodman band. Equally important, he was "instrumental" in the development of bebop in the forties via his participation in after hours jam sessions at Minton's in Harlem. Like a shooting star, his talent blazed for a brief period between 1939 and 1942 until he died at the tender age of 25. The number of guitarists who fell under Christian's pervasive influence is countless and still multiplying, with Tiny Grimes, Oscar Moore, Barney Kessel, George Barnes, Les Paul, Tal Farlow, and Herb Ellis being only some of the most prominent.

The next stylistic leap occurred in the late fifties when rumors of a fantastic new jazz guitarist, toiling in obscurity in Indianapolis, made their way east. Wes Montgomery, using his thumb rather than a plectrum, was absolutely dazzling in his speed and dexterity. He knew the Charlie Christian songbook in and out, but added his own extraordinary octave technique and bop blues sensibility to a style that became the benchmark for virtually all other jazz guitarists. Tired of playing long hours for short pay in the jazz clubs, Montgomery took a turn towards easy listening arrangements of pop tunes in the mid-sixties to the consternation of jazz purists and died too young at the age of 44 in 1968.

Concurrent with Montgomery's rise in the sixties was the sighting of yet another young man gobbling up acres of fingerboard. Combining the best of Charlie Christian and Wes, George Benson was literally playing his way out of R&B bands on his way to becoming even bigger and more popular than his predecessors. With superior chops and the longevity to let them develop and mature, he is arguably the most famous jazz guitarist of all time as well as one of the greatest.

George Benson was born March 22, 1943 in Pittsburgh, Pennsylvania. The precocious youngster discovered early on that he possessed a singing voice and actually made his public debut at age four at a Fourth of July show, leading to his nickname--"Little Georgie Benson." Hearing the records of Charlie Christian with the Benny Goodman band a few years later in his home lit his desire to play. His stepfather, Tom Collier, who had aspirations of playing professionally, owned an electric guitar that young George coveted. Since his hands were too small at this point, however, he had to settle for a ukulele instead. By the time he was eight, Benson was rewarded with a cheap guitar as Collier acknowledged his progress. A local producer noted his talents after seeing him perform on street corners and took him to New York. At the age of ten, Little Georgie Benson was inked to a short term contract with RCA Victor Records "X" label, and cut four sides of R&B music, including Ray Charles's "It Should Have Been Me." Only one single, "She Makes Me Mad," was released, and the experience added to Benson's notoriety back home, but Benson's strict stepfather saw the music as too much of a distraction and he took the guitar away.

Perhaps the absence of a strong, worthwhile avocation in his life had some effect; at age 15, Benson got in trouble and served six weeks in reform school. When he got out he joined the Altarrs, an R&B singing group started by a cousin. Wishing to play the guitar again as well as sing, Collier built George a homemade electric and amplification system for his use. By 17, he was singing and playing with the Altarrs, as they became one of the most popular groups in the area.

Within a year Benson was itching to have his own band. He formed a quintet whose repertoire consisted almost entirely of R&B, but he was starting to develop a real interest in jazz. Hearing *Jazz Winds from a New Direction* featuring Hank Garland and vibist Gary Burton spurred him on to further investigation. Before long the work of Charlie Parker, Charlie Christian, and Wes Montgomery turned him in a new bop direction, and he began seriously woodshedding on his axe along with frequenting jam sessions. Jazz guitarists like Grant Green and Eddie McFadden passing through Pittsburgh added their encouragement upon hearing his ability and intensity. In fact, fellow Pittsburghian Grant Green would go on to suggest he try his hand at being a session musician.

In 1961, however, Benson got his break through an unexpected opportunity. Hammond organist Brother Jack McDuff was passing through with his trio minus the guitarist. Benson was immediately recommended to fill in and he ended up "subbing" for the next three years while undergoing the most challenging phase of his musical career. Though he had a superb sense of time and a deep groove, his harmonic and melodic knowledge was lacking, and he did not read music. With McDuff's constant encouragement Benson studied hard and acquired the necessary skills. In the meantime he met jazz giants John Coltrane, Kenny Burrell, Jim Hall, and Wes Montgomery. Wes became virtually a mentor to the young, up and coming guitarist. Prestige Records took notice of his choice chops, and in 1964 Benson waxed *The New Boss Guitar Of George Benson With The Brother Jack McDuff Quartet.* The publicity and critical acclaim persuaded him to go it alone, and he formed his own quartet in 1965. Along with most other jazz musicians of the time, the group scuffled in the clubs until Columbia Records talent scout extraordinaire John Hammond heard him and signed him to the major label. Preferring to feature him as a vocalist during those trying times for jazz, Columbia had him sing several tunes on his two albums. In 1967, Benson left Columbia for Verve where he recorded two platters.

Still looking for an empathetic label, in 1968 he joined A&M Records where he became a stable mate with Wes Montgomery. Wes had interceded on his behalf with producer Herb Alpert, and Benson ended up making three albums for the new and promising label. His producer was Creed Taylor, who had engineered Wes's unqualified commercial success by having him play pop tunes with ear-pleasing octaves. A similar path was taken with Benson (to the same critical consternation that followed Montgomery's "sellout") and when Taylor split in 1970 to form his own CTI label, Benson was taken along for the ride.

The concept of CTI Records was revolutionary. Instead of treating jazz as some esoteric art reserved for the cognoscenti, Taylor approached it with a pop sensibility. He got the best young jazzmen around, had them play standards, contemporary tunes, and originals, and sweetened the arrangements with orchestral backing. He then wrapped the music in visually striking, glossy artwork. The results were amazing. CTI records sold ten times the amount of most previous jazz releases.

Benson stayed with the label for six years, recording an album per annum. *White Rabbit* from 1972 was nominated for a Grammy, and Benson was accorded the honor of playing on Miles Davis's *Miles in the Sky*. The trumpet master offered him a spot in his band, which included at that time Herbie Hancock, Wayne Shorter, Ron Carter, and Tony Williams. Benson turned it down as he was satisfied with the financial remuneration from CTI, but he was also starting to chafe under Creed Taylor's creative restraints. When his contract with CTI was up for renewal in 1976, he signed with Warner Brothers.

The major labels were starting to acknowledge the wider acceptance of jazz that was growing out of fusion and the popularity of artists like Wes Montgomery and George Benson. With a sympathetic producer like Tony LiPuma, Benson had much more input than he had at CTI and promptly took advantage of it by bringing in his friend Phil Upchurch on rhythm guitar. LiPuma, in what can only be described as a stroke of genius, encouraged Benson to sing again and suggested "This Masquerade" by Leon Russell as his choice. *Breezin'* came out in 1976 and scored in the Top Ten pop charts based almost solely on the vocal number. It went platinum, selling millions of copies and received three Grammys. *In Flight* from 1977 followed suit in sales and awards. The formula of jazz, pop, and R&B with Benson's suave, satiny vocals and nimble fretwork proved a huge success all the way through to 1980's *Give Me the Night*, produced by Quincy Jones.

The eighties saw continued commercial success as Benson replayed the formula begun in the late seventies. Unfortunately, his guitar was becoming featured less and less, and his long term, hardcore jazz fans felt neglected. Beginning with *Tenderly*, a fine album of standards cut in 1989, and then *Big Boss Band* with the Count Basie band, he got back on track with his instrument. Throughout the nineties he has balanced all the elements of his talent into a commercially and critically successful phase of his long and productive career.

All the techniques, funky phrasing, and hip melodic ideas of George Benson are here for your delectation. Smoky, low down blues, bop classics, and modern pop all mix together for a comprehensive overview of this brilliant artist's majestic contribution to the magical language of jazz.

The Guitars of George Benson

George Benson has played a variety of fine jazz "boxes" over the years. These have included a Gibson Super 400, Gibson L5CES, Gibson L5C, D'Angelico New Yorker, Guild Starfire XII, Guild George Benson Custom (based on the George Barnes Acousti Lectric), and Ibanez George Benson signature GB10 and GB20 guitars.

A Note on the Transcriptions

Every effort has been made to notate the songs as accurately as possible, as in all Hal Leonard Corporation publications. In terms of the tab, however, the reader should realize that, generally speaking, the fingerings are a guide to how the artist *may* have played that song on the particular day the recording was made. Great improvisers like George Benson often have more than one way of playing the exact same passage of notes. In addition, as their playing evolves over the years, subtle fingering changes tend to occur naturally.

Affirmation

(Breezin', 1976)
By Jose Feliciano

Written by Jose Feliciano, "Affirmation" is typical of the type of Latin-jazz tunes that have afforded the genre a wider audience. Gently swaying rhythms reminiscent of sambas past, cascading electronic keyboards, and soothing strings all contributed to a billowy cushion for the soloist. Benson was already a master at negotiating bebop changes at breakneck tempos. "Blowing" over one or two-chord vamps, as often found on these numbers, presented little technical challenge, and he often let his "fingers do the walking."

FIGURE 1

Study

The 8-measure, unaccompanied intro with pickup consists of a vamp from Em9 to Bm7sus4. Each chord change is two measures long within which Benson combines scale runs and chords. The key of D is notated with Bm functioning as the relative minor; therefore the B Aeolian mode is employed exclusively with the C natural (♭9th) used as a grace note in measure 5. One voicing of the Bm7sus4 is played in measures 4 and 8, while Em9 followed by Em7sus4 appears in measures 3 and 6.

The phrasing in the intro is a wonderful example of how to maintain interest with basic chord changes (i–iv) by dynamically varying the rhythms in every measure.

Performance

After the pickup measure, Benson plays the chords on either beat 1 or 2 of each new change. Notice how he plans his fingering so that the last note before each new chord is a note included in that chord voicing. For the Em9 chords in measures 2 and 6, use your ring finger to play the F♯ note on beat 1 and then try making a small barre with it to catch the D (♭7th) and F♯ (9th) notes in the chord itself. For the Bm7sus4 chord in measures 4 and 8, end on the E note in the preceding measures with your pinky and then apply that finger to the chord.

Measure 8 contains a longer, faster run with 32nd as well as 16th notes. As it involves several position shifts, try using the following finger recommendations to start on each string: String 6 = index, string 4 = index, string 3 = ring, string 2 = middle, string 1 = index on E. Then slide from F♯ to A with the ring, play the F♯ with the ring, the E with the index, and the D on string 2 with the pinky.

Fig. 1

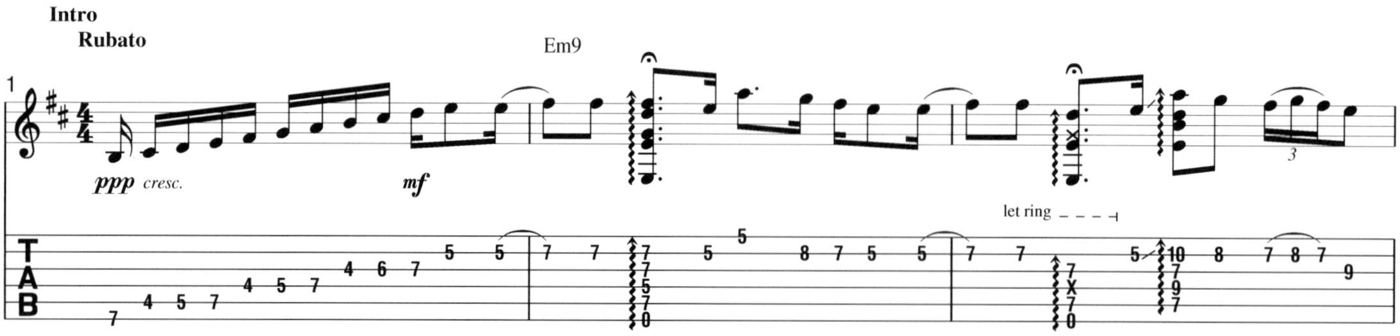

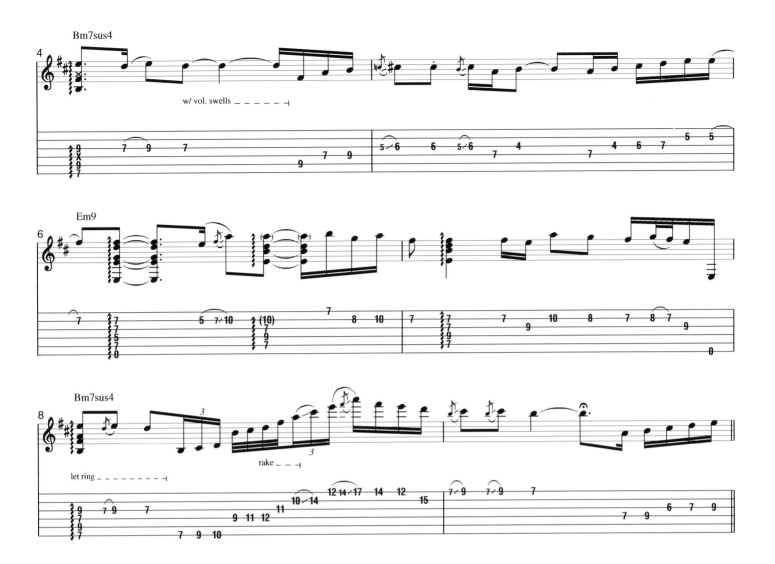

FIGURE 2

Study

The outro solo finds Benson slapping chords, triads, double stops, and octaves with joyous abandon over a one chord (Bm7) vamp to the fade out. He phrases with sophisticated syncopation, varying the rhythms in every measure. Inasmuch as the harmony is static, Benson constantly switches from chordal forms consonant and dissonant to D. The double stops include funky 4ths and "Asian-sounding" 5ths, while the octaves, a Benson trademark courtesy of Wes Montgomery, often have the 5th (another GB trademark) inserted to provide additional harmony.

In particular, notice the F octaves (with 5ths) in measures 11 onward that lift the spirit of the solo as the tune fades. Relative to the Bm harmony, F is the ♭5th, a hip dissonance that engenders cool musical tension, especially when it is repeated so many times. Dig that the ♭5th has been called the "defining harmony of the 20th century."

Performance

Virtually every form is cued with the index finger being the lowest note. Besides providing easy access to all the forms, it allows for efficient damping of the string between the octaves by flattening the index until it lightly touches (mutes) the unwanted string. Some players use their thumb and index fingers to pluck standard octaves, or the pick and middle finger. Considering the tempo and speed with which Benson moves between positions, the pick alone in conjunction with string damping is really the only choice.

Fig. 2

Billie's Bounce
(Bill's Bounce)
(Giblet Gravy, 1968)
By Charlie Parker

"Billie's Bounce" was written by Charlie Parker and originally recorded by the bebop alto giant in 1945. It should have been spelled "Billy's" instead, since it was named in honor of booking agent Billy Shaw, not Billie Holiday as is often mistaken. A bopping 12-bar blues, it sports a rippling head that is beloved by guitarists while presenting a hefty technical challenge.

"Bird" was one of Benson's prime influences and founts of inspiration. Fully up to the task, he breezes through the head of "Billie's Bounce" and romps through the blues changes with his usual cool assurance while exhibiting genuine gutbucket attitude.

FIGURE 1

Study

The 12-bar head contains standard jazz chord substitutions. In measures 7–10 (where the changes would normally be I–I–V–IV), I–VI–ii–V is used as a substitute progression. The melody is derived from a composite of the F Mixolydian mode, F dominant bebop scale, and F blues scale with the addition of the ♯5th and ♭9th. The Mixolydian mode contains the root, 2nd, 3rd, 4th, 5th, 6th, and b7th notes. The dominant bebop scale is identical except that it adds the major 7th as a passing tone in between the ♭7th and octave, and was a favorite of beboppers (hence the name!) during the era.

Bird composed the head with a keen ear to outlining the changes, especially the VI7 (D7), ii (Gm7), and V7 (C7) chords. In measure 8 (D7), the C, A, G, F♯, E♭, and C♯ notes function as the ♭7th, 5th, 4th, 3rd, ♭9th, and major 7th of D. In measure 9 (Gm7), the D, G, F♯, and B♭ notes act as the 5th, root, major 7th, and ♭3rd of G, suggesting a G harmonic minor scale. In measure 10 (C7), the F, E, and D notes function as the 4th, 3rd, and 9th of C.

The I (F) chord changes emphasize the root (F) and 6th (D) along with the classic blues move of the ♭3rd (A♭) to the 3rd (A). Over the IV (B♭) chord, the ♭7th (A♭) is played in addition to the root (B♭) and 5th (F).

Performance

Two "blues boxes" could be seen as the fingering positions. The first one would be between frets 3 and 6 and resembles a G blues scale with the addition of the Ab and A notes below at frets 1 and 2. This will suffice for all the changes except the VI7 (D7) in measure 8. Try shifting your hand position from measure 7 so that your pinky plays the C note at fret 5 and your index finger plays the A note at fret 2. This forms a box that looks similar to an F♯ blues scale.

Fig. 1

 Melody (Guitar and Bass Unison)

FIGURE 2

Study

Four choruses into his solo, Benson is "strutting his stuff" through the changes. In measures 1–4 (I7–IV7–I7), he uses the F Mixolydian mode with the addition of the ♭9th (G♭), the bluesy ♭5th (B), and the ♭6th (D♭). In measures 5 and 6 (IV7), he shifts to the B♭ Ionian mode where the natural 7th (A) punctuates the major, rather than dominant quality, of the B♭7 chord change. In measure 7 (I7), Benson obliquely acknowledges the F7 with the 9th and sus4 for tension. Note that the sus4 (B♭) is the ♯5th of D7♯5(♯9) in measure 8, where he glides into the D blues scale (see the ♭3rd) with the ♯5 and ♯9 notes. In measure 9 (ii), he incorporates the G Dorian mode along with the tangy ♭5th. Measure 10 (V7) utilizes the C Mixolydian mode with emphasis on the melodic 3rd and ♭7th notes.

Measures 11 and 12 of the turnaround move harmonically iii–VI7–ii–V7 as a substitute sequence for I7–V7. Benson judiciously chooses the root and ♭3rd (Am7), sus4, ♭3rd/♯9th, and ♭7th (D7♯9), and ♭7th, 5th, and 9th (C7) notes to outline the changes.

Inventive, swinging phrasing is displayed as usual as Benson never plays two measures the same rhythmically. Where a lesser guitarist would just peel off measure after measure of eighth notes, Benson always leaves significant musical rests.

Performance

Benson works "vertically" with the F Mixolydian mode (F–G–A–B♭–C–D–E♭) at fret 8 as his base. This allows him to easily access the B♭ (fret 6) and C (fret 8) scales while carefully selecting notes from the F major scale for the other chord changes.

Fig. 2

FIGURE 3

Study

Chorus 7 finds Benson mixing double stops, double-stop bends, and swift single-note lines as he begins to build towards his chordal climax (Figure 4). In measures 1, 3, and 4 (I), he emphasizes F/B♭ (root/sus4) and C/A♭ (5th/♭3rd) as tension-producers that resolve (eventually) to the root. Measures 2, 5, and 6 (IV) use the D, C, and G notes from the F Mixolydian mode as the 3rd, 9th, and 6th of B♭. In addition, the F/B♭ and C/A♭ double stops (functioning as the 5th/root and 9th/♭7th, respectively) are employed.

Measures 8–12 contain a virtuosic string of eighth notes outlining the changes. As in Figure 2, Benson negotiates the changes from the altered F Mixolydian mode at fret 8. The skill with which he plucks (pun intended!) the correct scale degrees over each change, at a brisk tempo, is nothing short of amazing. Over the D7♭9 he emphasizes the root (D), ♭7th (C), and ♭9th (E♭); over the Gm7 he emphasizes the sus4th (C), 9th (A), root (G), and ♭3rd (B♭); and over the C7 he emphasizes the 5th (G), 9th (D), 3rd (E), and ♭7th (B♭). In the turnaround he plays the ♭6th, 5th, and ♭5th (F7), the 5th, ♭5th, and spicy ♭3rd (D7), the ♭6th, ♭5th, and sus4 (Gm7), and the root, 3rd, and 5th (C7).

Be hip to the fact that all those "altered" tones (♭5th, ♭6th, ♭9th, etc.) are what separates the "twangers" from the "jazzers!"

Performance

Benson tosses in a couple of R&B techniques from his funky "old days" in Pittsburgh and his days with Jack McDuff. In measures 3 and 5, he "smears" a bluesy, quarter-step double-stop bend of the notes C/A♭ with his middle and index fingers. In measure 4, he hammers from the B♭ to the B♮ with his index and middle fingers while sustaining the F with his ring finger.

Fig. 3

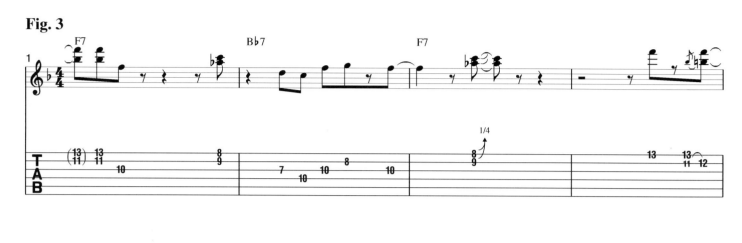

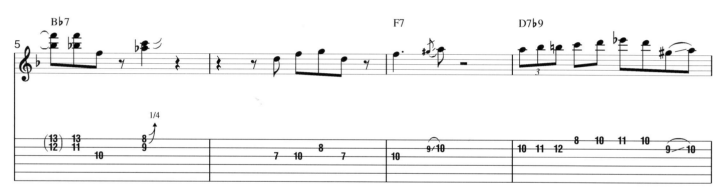

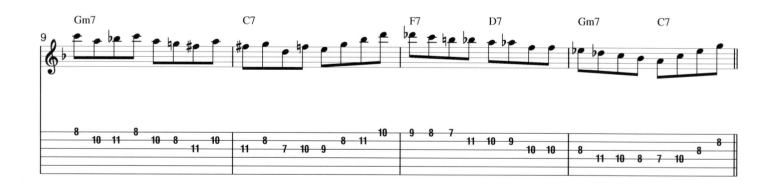

FIGURE 4

Study

The penultimate tenth solo chorus builds to a climax with Benson whipping chords and octaves back and forth with glee. As befits his superior skills and vision, his choice of voicings and rhythmic application functions as both accompaniment and solo as the piano rests. Harmonically he blends in alternate voicings as well as cool substitutions: F#9sus4, F#13sus4, F#9, and F#7#5 for the I7 (F7) in measures 2–4, and Bbm9 for the IV7 (Bb7) in measure 6. Benson also regularly extends the minor seventh chords (Am7 and Gm7) to minor ninths, as well as implying 6/9 chords in measures 10 (F#) and 12 (E6/9 to F6/9 as a pickup into the following solo chorus). Note that the same voicing when applied to a minor seventh chord change (Am7 in measure 11) implies am Am11.

Of particular interest is the second inversion 9sus4 (F# and F) in measures 2 and 3 that also functions as a minor eleven voicing (Gm11) in measure 12. Likewise, the first inversion of the Gm7 on beat 2 in measure 9 follows the third inversion nicely.

Performance

As mentioned previously, Benson often leads into his scale and chord forms with his index finger. Keeping this in mind will facilitate logical and practical fingerings for the chords in Figure 4. Therefore, all of the barres in measures 3, 6, 7, 8, and 9 use the index finger. The chords that require double-barres in measures 10–12 use the index and ring fingers.

Having a thorough knowledge of the fingerings is essential for the proper performance of this passage, as the syncopation requires fast strums and position shifts.

Fig. 4

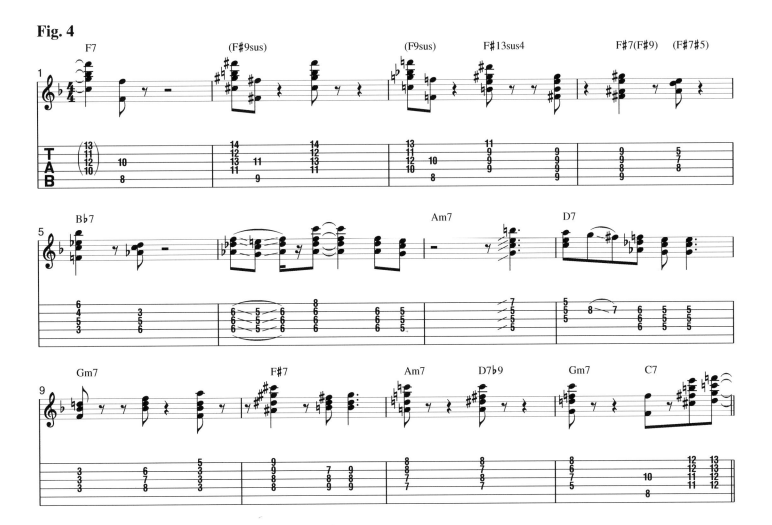

Breezin'

(Breezin', 1976)
Words and Music by Bobby Womack

Written by soul man Bobby Womack and recorded several years earlier by the contemporary gypsy guitarist Gabor Szabo, "Breezin'" did for pop jazz what the Beatles had done for pop rock a decade before. It showed for all the world to see that a light, Latin groove, combined with a simple, catchy hook could turn "strings" into gold. Though Wes Montgomery had tried a similar, successful experiment along the same lines in the late sixties, the sheer sales volume and awards involved was unprecedented.

"This Masquerade" was the breakout hit from the album due in large part to George Benson's remarkable vocals, but "Breezin'" opened the floodgates for all the "lite" fusion and jazz that followed. Purists were not amused, but the public ate it up and the musicians had a decent payday for a change.

FIGURE 1

Study

This intro cast the die for a good deal of popular jazz that followed. After a I–♭III–V–♭III–I (measures 1–5) sequence of candy apple major 7ths in 3/4 time, it settles into a 4-measure vamp in 4/4 cut time. Measures 6–13 move I–vi–ii–IV two times (D–Bm7–Em7–G/A) as Benson strums each chord and then plays a fill (except for measure 6 where he rests and measure 13 where he continues strumming the G/A chord). The run connecting D to Bm7 contains the 5th, root, 2nd, and 3rd notes from the D major scale. The hammer-on lick that precedes the Em7 chord in measure 7 emphasizes the 5th and ♭7th notes of the Bm7 chord. The run that connects the Em7 to G/A includes the 5th, root, 2nd, and ♭3rd from the E Dorian mode.

Measures 14–17 contain the same slightly altered sequence (Dmaj9 instead of D, and Em9 instead of Em7) of chords. Over the top Benson strums sweet double stops relative to each chord: E/A (9th/5th) for Dmaj9, D/B (♭3rd/root) for Bm7, F♯/D (9th/♭7th) for Em9, and E/C♯ (6th/♯4th of G, but 5th/3rd of A). This vamp is repeated five more times until the verse.

Performance

Though they should be self-explanatory, the proper fingerings are vital to the smooth joining of runs to chords. For the D–Bm7 measure (6), play the F♯ with your ring finger so you are in position for the Bm7 voicing. Barre the hammer-on lick in measure 7 with your index finger so that you can play the E note on string 4 with the same finger for the Em7 chord. For the Em7–G/A measure (8), play the G note with your pinky so that you are in position for the G/A chord.

All of the double stops should be played with the ring and index fingers.

Fig. 1

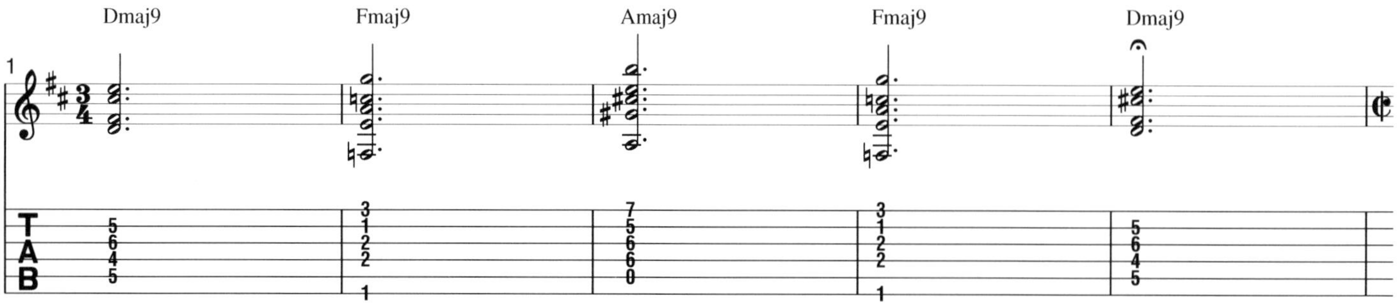

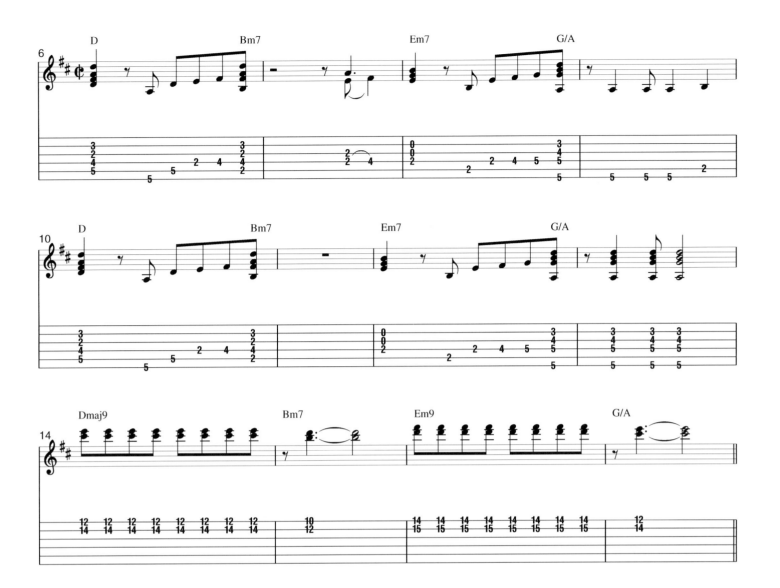

FIGURE 2

Study

The verse melody consists of the extended intro chords combined into an 8-measure phrase, cycled four times, for a 32-measure verse. With the D Ionian mode (D major scale) as his source, Benson constructs a simple melodic line leaving plenty of musical space. Figure 2 shows measures 1–8 of the verse melody with the pickup measure from the intro (G/A) included. In measure 1 of the verse (Dmaj9), he decorates the 5th (A) with a hammer-on and pull-off to and from the 6th (B). He rests over the Bm7 and then plays the same lick from measure 1 over the Em9, where the notes now function as sus4 and 5th. Over G/A, Benson uses a descending run with major 7th (F♯), 5th (D), and 3rd (B) that resolves to the 5th of D (A) in measure 5. Once again he rests over the Bm7, then plays a series of hammer-ons and pull-offs containing the sus4 and 5th over the Em9. In measure 9 (G/A), he plays virtually the same ascending run to lead back into the next 8-measure increment.

Striving for a very consonant, melodic "inside sound," Benson picks on 5ths and 6ths almost exclusively, along with the sweet 3rd and the semi-sweet sus4.

Performance

Of little challenge technically, Figure 2 requires a soft, even touch. The hammer-ons and pull-offs, of course, should be executed with the index and ring fingers.

Fig. 2

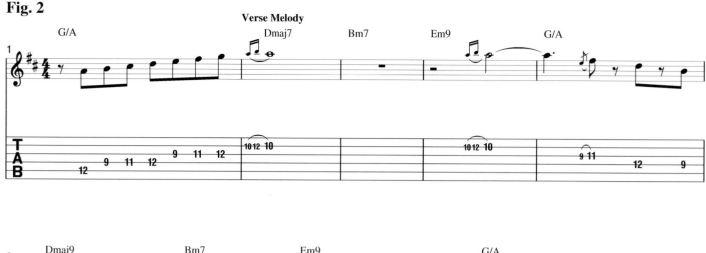

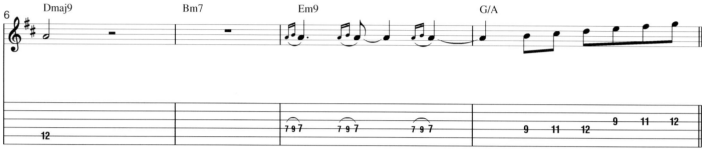

FIGURE 3

Study

The B-Verse is approached more as a solo. In fact, Benson even manages to generate a little "heat" with some sassy octaves near the climax! Measures 1–8 consist of two, almost identical, four-measure phrases. Slipping into the B relative minor "box" at fret 7, Benson plays the root (D) and 6th (B) notes over the Dmaj9, the ♭7th (A), root (B), ♭3rd (D), and 5th (F♯) notes over the Bm7, the ♭7th (D) and 9th (F♯) notes over the Em9, and the 2nd (A), 3rd (B), 5th (D), and 6th (E) notes over the G/A chord.

Beginning on beat 4 of measure 8, however, he starts squeezing in slightly rambunctious octaves (some with the 5th inserted in between the two octave notes). In measure 9 (Dmaj9), he plays the root and 6th. In measure 10 (Bm7), he repeats virtually the same single notes from measures 2 and 6 before sliding from the ♭5th on beat 4 to the root in measure 11 (Em9), followed by the ♭7th, 9th, and sus4. In measure 12 (G/A), Benson plays the root, ♭7th, major 7th, 9th, and 3rd. Measures 13–16 are similar to measures 9–12. On beats 2, 3, and 4 of measure 16, he plays the same D Ionian mode run over G/A that he used in the pickup measure of Figure 2.

In keeping with the "tone" of "Breezin'," Benson sticks mainly to the stable 5ths and 6ths with the bluesy ♭7ths and 9ths included for a little aural stimulation.

Performance

As all of the octaves are either on strings 3 and 1, or 4 and 2, and require the use of the index and pinky fingers, it is easy to add the 5th with the ring finger. When playing the octaves minus the 5th, mute the string in between by lightly touching it with the underside of your index finger.

Fig. 3

B-Verse

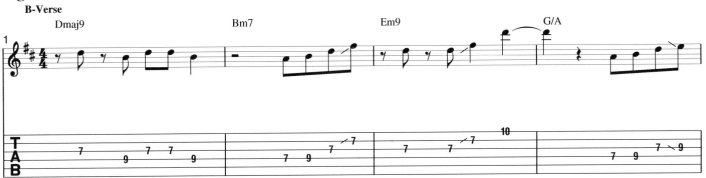

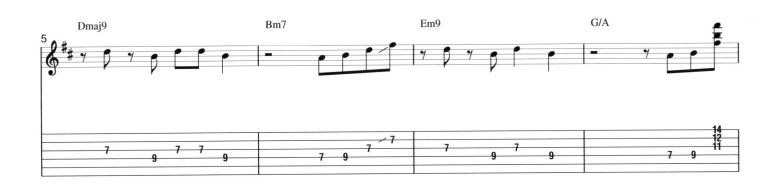

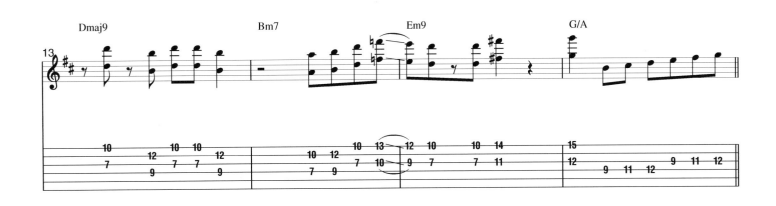

FIGURE 4

Study

Measures 41–47 of the solo show Benson's ability to work "down home blues" bends and other "simple" ideas into a pop jazz tune. Like the rest of "Breezin'," the solo also consists of the same 4-measure chord sequence. Again focusing his attention on the B relative minor scale around fret 7, Benson bends the F one-half step to F♯ over the Dmaj9 and Bm7 where it functions as the 3rd of D and 5th of B. He also bangs on the D note repeatedly (like a honking R&B sax man) as dynamic contrast to the slithery bends, as it is a common tone in each of the four chords.

In measure 48 (G/A), Benson exposes his thrilling speed briefly as he rips down the G Mixolydian mode (using the ♭7th for tension) over the G/A, ending on a C♯, rather than a C♮. The C♯ functions as the leading tone (major 7) into the next measure of Dmaj9.

Performance

The F should be bent with the ring finger, and the D note on string 3 should be played with the index finger. This will allow a convenient anchoring point from which to nab the other notes. Start the run over G/A with your index finger and follow through with a logical fingering, applying one finger per fret in the 4-fret span.

Fig. 4

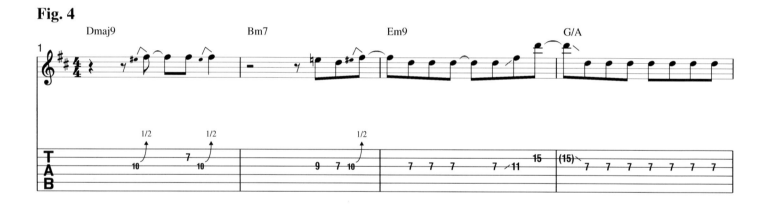

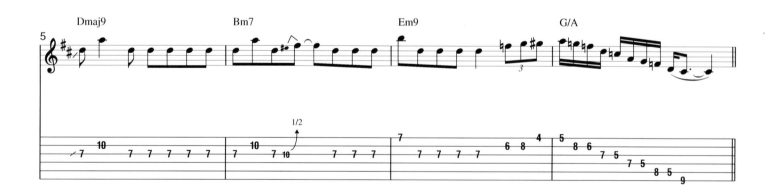

The Cooker
(The George Benson Cookbook, 1966)
By George Benson

The title of this scorching 12-bar blues is no idle boast. The boiler would be more appropriate, as George Benson bounces his pick from string to string like a ping pong ball. He has been quoted as saying there was a time when even he would look down in amazement at his flying fingers. Suffice it to say that recording "The Cooker" may well have been one of those occurrences.

With a half dozen albums under his belt by 1966, Benson was getting to the point where he could feel comfortable mixing jazz standards, vocal tunes, originals, blues, and a little rock 'n' roll together on his recordings. Given his R&B background and admiration for firmly rooted, bluesy jazz guitarists like Charlie Christian and Wes Montgomery, however, it is no surprise that he felt especially at home working out on a "cooking" 12-bar progression.

FIGURE 1

Study

The 12-bar progression under the head uses the following arrangement: I (4 measures), IV (2 measures), I (2 measures), ii (1 measure), ♭II (1 measure), and I (2 measures). Notice that the A13 chord in measure 10 is a tri-tone substitute for the E♭ dominant chord, which would normally occur at that point in the progression.

The stop-time head has Benson and baritone saxophonist Ronnie Cuber riffing in unison. Benson signals each chord change (except the B♭m7 in measure 9) with a partial dominant voicing. Following each chord "hit" on the I and IV chords is a two-measure run in the A♭ blues scale. The run is identical each time except for the last note, which alternates between A♭ and G♭.

The ii (B♭m7) change includes a run in the B♭ Dorian mode that resolves to the root, while the ♭II (A13) features one in the A Mixolydian mode that ends on the 3rd (C♯). As the C♯ (or D♭) could be seen as the 4th of A♭, it helps to lead the ear back to the tonic chord.

Note: The 12-bar progression changes to A♭ (4 measures), D♭ (2 measures), A♭ (2 measures), B♭m7 (2 measures), and A♭ (2 measures) for the solo section.

Performance

Standard blues scale fingerings apply throughout the head. Though the runs are relatively simple, due to the headlong tempo, fast, accurate down-and-up pick strokes are a necessity. In addition, the chords should be muted with the heel of the right hand immediately after striking them with the pick.

Fig. 1

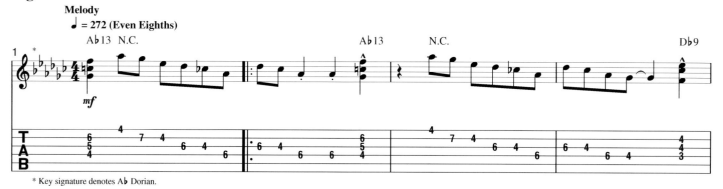

* Key signature denotes A♭ Dorian.

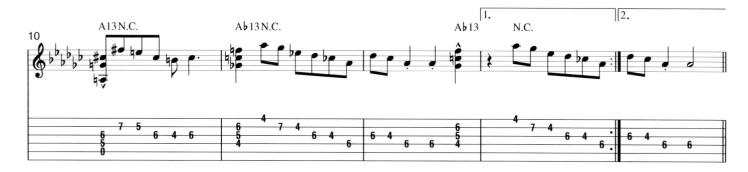

FIGURE 2

Study

Benson's first chorus is a marvelous lesson in how to grab the listener by the ears and not let go. In measures 1 and 2 of the I chord, he emphasizes the pointy ♭5th (D) in conjunction with the 6th (F) and ♭7th (F♯). Following in measure 3 he moves his 2-note fingering pattern on string 2 up the neck to include the ♯5th (E), root (A♭ or G♯), ♭7th (G♭), and 9th (B♭), resolving to the root in measure 4. The unusual and syncopated phrasing pattern in measures 1–3 (a quarter note followed by two eighth notes), along with the bold note selection contributes to a heightened sense of giddy anticipation.

In measure 5 (IV), Benson shifts to the D♭ Mixolydian mode and establishes his key change with the 3rd (F), root (D♭), and ♭7th (C♭ or B). He follows up in measure 6 with the 9th (E♭), ♭3rd (E, from the D♭ blues scale), root, and ♭7th. Without coming up for air, he modulates back into the A♭ Mixolydian mode around the 9th position in measures 7 and 8. And, while he starts and ends his phrase with the root and 3rd (again establishing tonality with his key change), he peppers the eighth-note run with ♯5ths and ♭9ths.

Measures 9 and 10 (iim7) find Benson in the B♭ Dorian mode. Dig how he creates bluesy tension with the 9th (C), 4th (E♭), ♭7th (A♭), 5th (F), and ♭3rd (D♭) notes before resolving to the root (B♭) in measure 10. Then, notice how he lays on the major 7th (A) as a passing tone to the A♭ note in measure 11 (I). After all that audio information, he rests in measure 12 before picking up the gauntlet once again in the next chorus.

Performance

At this tempo, logical fingering choices remain essential. One rule of thumb is to begin each measure with the proper finger and the rest of the notes should follow accordingly. In measures 1, 2, 3, 5, 7, 8, 9, 10, and 11, lead in with your index finger. In measures 4 and 6, use your ring finger.

Fig. 2

* Key signature denotes A♭ Mixolydian.

FIGURE 3

Study

Benson's 7th solo chorus consists of one gravity-defying, bendy lick repeated for the entire 12 measures. With the E♭ as a pedal point, he bends the D up one half step to match the E♭, followed by the C♭ (B) bent a slick, "true blues" quarter step. The E♭ and C♭ harmonize with the A♭ (5th and ♭3rd), D♭ (9th and ♭7th), and B♭ (4th and ♭9th) chord changes and create a terrific amount of musical tension.

Performance

Use your index finger for the E♭, your pinky for the D, and your middle finger for the C♭ note.

Fig. 3

Solo (7th Chorus)

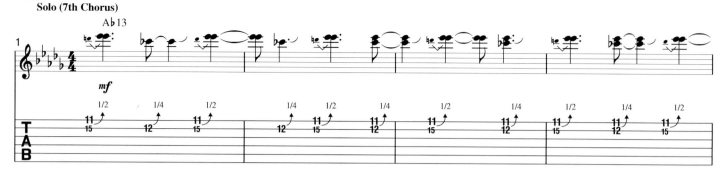

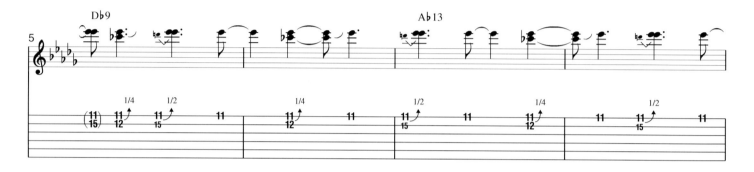

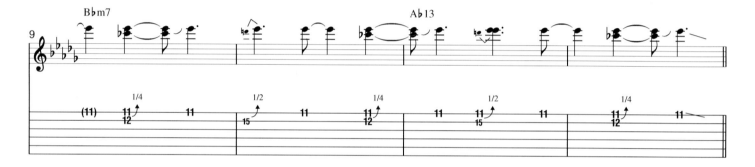

FIGURE 4

Study

Similar to Figure 3, Benson repeats two licks for the bulk of the 10th chorus. In measures 1–6, he repeats a 3-note phrase consisting of C♯, D, and E♭. Due to the fact that he plays this as steady eighth notes in each measure, the starting point for each sequence of notes changes in measures 1–3, then repeats again in measure 4. Be sure to see that the sequence begins on the D note before settling in. Again, this is a highly effective tension-producing device in which the sound of the pattern is actually more important than the literal harmony produced by the individual notes.

In measure 7, Benson abruptly halts the breath-taking onslaught and inserts a picaresque blues lick consisting of the ♭3rd slid to the 3rd and ending on the "dissonant" ♭3rd. After resting in measure 8 (a rest for the listener as well!), he begins a new 3-note pattern over the iim7 change consisting of the ♭9th (B), 9th (C), and ♭7th (A♭). In measure 11 (I), he semi-resolves to the melodic 6th (F) and rests in measure 12.

Performance

Use your index, middle and ring fingers for the pattern in measures 1–6. Try strict down-and-up pick strokes. Use your pinky (for the legato slide) and your index finger for the A♭ note in measures 9 and 10, also with alternating down-and-up pick strokes.

Fig. 4

Solo (10th Chorus)

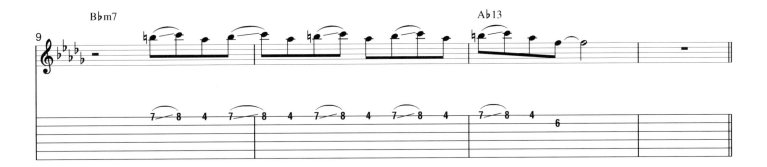

FIGURE 5

Study

As a dynamic interlude to the relentless forward motion of "The Cooker," Benson presents a stop-time progression in the 13th chorus. The way he builds momentum in just 12 measures is nothing short of remarkable. In measures 1–4 (I), he starts with a double stop of a ♭3rd (C♭/E♭) to establish the A♭ tonality and follows with a major 2nd (A♭/G♭) in measure 2. In measure 3, he squeezes out two, slow (relatively!) unison bends of a 5th and in measure 4 he plays a descending run down the A♭ minor pentatonic scale that resolves to the root.

In measure 5, Benson trots out a classic IV chord move with the D♭ and C♭ (B) from the A♭ blues scale functioning as the root and ♭7th of D♭. In measure 6, he "takes it up a notch" with a quicksilver pair of eighth notes and triplets based on an altered E♭ diminished scale and a D♭ triad.

After reestablishing his A♭ tonality with the root note, Benson rips through the altered A♭ Mixolydian mode in measures 7 and 8. He plays in a more "horizontal" fashion on the top three strings, emphasizing the critical 3rd while including the ♯5th and ♭9th notes.

Moving down chromatically from the ♭9th of A♭ (A) to the ♭7th of B♭m7 (A♭) in measure 9, Benson cruises into the B♭ harmonic minor scale with its characteristic major 7th (A) degree through to measure 10. Mashing down on the turbo-thruster, he starts a stunning chromatic sequence from the 9th (C) at fret 8 on string 1 that climbs steadily to the ♭9th (A) of A♭ at fret 17 in measure 11. Kicking in the afterburners, he zooms down through the A♭ Mixolydian mode (with the inclusion of the ♭3rd from the A♭ blues scale), arriving at the root and resolution on the last beat of measure 12.

Performance

The only way to accurately learn a solo chorus of this complexity and speed is to proceed very slowly at first. With so much movement up and down the fingerboard, it is fruitless to decree one fingering system. Therefore, work out patterns that are practical and make use of all four fingers. One example would be measure 6 (IV). Try using an arpeggio-type fingering where your pinky plays the Eb, your ring finger the Gb, your middle finger the Bb, and your index finger the Db. Be aware that, unless you have an especially large hand, you will have to adjust your position between the Eb and the Gb due to the span involved.

Fig. 5

Easy Living
(The New Boss Guitar of George Benson, 1964)
Theme from the Paramount Picture EASY LIVING
Words and Music by Leo Robin and Ralph Rainger

It may be a coincidence that "Easy Living" is most often associated with Billie Holiday, one of the legendary singers in jazz. Though George Benson is probably capable of providing a credible vocal rendition, it is his guitar "voice" that speaks so beautifully on this moving version. With the most unobtrusive backing (including, uncharacteristically, Hammond organist Brother Jack McDuff on piano), this lovely ballad is mainly a vehicle for Benson's under appreciated chord melody technique.

FIGURE 1

Study

"Easy Living" is a classic 32-measure song consisting of two 8-measure sections (A and B) arranged AABA. Benson harmonizes it extensively, but the two progressions could be seen as follows:

A Section
1. I–iii
2. ii
3. I
4. IV–iv
5. I–iii
6. ii–V7
7. I–VI7
8. ii–V7

The "B" section, starting in measure 17, appears to make a key change to D♭ due to a chromatic modulation in measure 16 from Fm9 to Em9 and E♭m9. (Note: If you think of the D♭ as the relative major of B♭m, then the B♭m could be seen as the iv of F, a common chord upon which to start a bridge or "B" section.) The E♭m9 then begins functioning as the ii of D♭ so that the A♭13 that follows is seen as the V, with resolution to the I (D♭) in measure 17. This series of "ii-V-I" changes is a powerful tool for producing forward motion in jazz progressions and can be seen as the basis for section "B," eventually resolving back to the V7 (C7) of F in measure 24.

B Section
17. I–vi
18. ii–V7
19. I–vi
20. ii–V7
21. I–vi
22. vi (could be seen as iv of F)
23. ii (of F)
24. V7 (of F)

Benson's artistry shows itself in the chord voicings, chord substitutions, and melodic single-note lines that he brings to bear on the song. In measure 2, he harmonizes the melody with the top note of each chord. The B7#9 in measure 3 is a hip tri-tone substitute for the I7 (F7) chord. Measure 4 is an excellent example of chords hitting on the downbeats (1, 3, and 4) with single-note lines of varying lengths following in between. This is one of the most effective ways of producing a full sound on the solo guitar that implies the presence of one or two additional instruments.

In measure 6, Benson uses a common tone (A on string 2) to bind the Gm9, C7sus4, and C13 chords together. Measures 7 and 8 have him voicing his chords and melody lines on the top two strings for a tightly focused sound that brings the first "A" section to a climax and makes the return to the beginning of the melody in measure 9 more dramatic. Again, as a dramatic, dynamic device, Benson begins the "B" section in measure 17 with a sparse arrangement of the two basic chords interspersed with the repeating 5th (Ab) of the Dbmaj7, and the root, b7th, and b3rd notes of the Bbm7 chord. This is brilliantly followed in measure 18 with a ringing series of m9th chords moving to the V7 and ending with a melody line embellished with a hammer-on and pull-off.

Measures 21 and 22 contain the longest string of single notes in Figure 1. After the triple-stop Bbm7 voicing on beat 3, Benson plays the b7th (Ab), 5th (F), root (Bb), 9th (C), and 6th (G) notes, with the Bbm 1st inversion triad inserted on beat 1 of measure 22 to shore up the harmony.

All of the single-note lines throughout are derived from the mode or scale directly related to the chord, from the actual chord tones, or a combination thereof.

Performance

As indicated, "Easy Living" should be played fingerstyle. Use your thumb to strum the chords, and a combination of thumb, index, and middle fingers for the single-note lines. As for the left-hand fingerings, try to cue the single notes from the chord fingerings. For example, play the Bbmaj7 chord in measure 4 with your index, ring, pinky, and middle fingers—low to high. Start the run on string 3 with your middle finger, followed by your ring, middle, and index fingers. In measure 7, play the Fadd9 chord with your middle, index, ring, and pinky fingers. Use your pinky for the C at fret 13 and your index for the D at fret 10.

Fig. 1

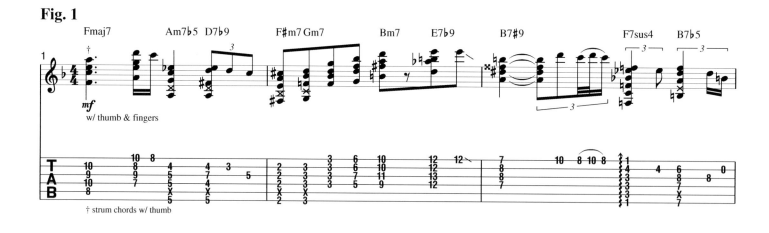

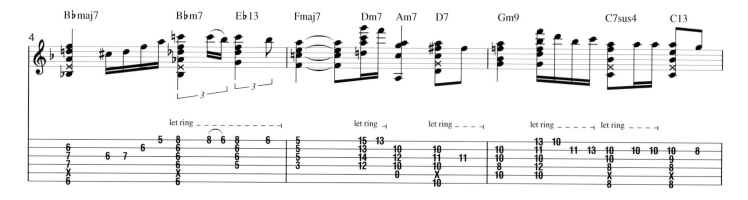

Gentle Rain

(Beyond The Blue Horizon, 1971)

from the Motion Picture THE GENTLE RAIN
Music by Luiz Bonfa   Words by Matt Dubey

Beyond The Blue Horizon was George Benson's first venture with Creed Taylor and his upstart CTI label. Three of the five compositions were Benson originals along with Miles Davis's "So What," and "The Gentle Rain" from the movie of the same title. Written by Brazilian bossa nova baron Luiz Bonfa of "Manha de Carnival" fame, it perfectly captures the lilting rhythms and minor key tonalities favored by Taylor.

Benson was accompanied on his maiden voyage by bassist Ron Carter and drummer Jack DeJohnette. Other talented contemporary musicians would later join the three young lions in the early seventies.

FIGURE 1

Study

Shades of Wes! The second time through the melody Benson caresses moody octaves on strings 5 and 3 for roughly half of the 22 measures. With the key signature as C, relative to Am, he bases his note selection almost entirely on the A Aeolian mode with two exceptions. In measure 10, the F♯ (6th) is played in lieu of the F♮ (♭6th), and in measure 11, the B♭ (♭9th) appears instead of the B♮ (9th). Understand that the F♯, however, functions as the 5th of B and that the B♭ coincides with the (naturally occurring) ♭5th of Em7♭5. Also an exception are the C and B♭ bass notes (measures 5 and 6) that function as anticipation of the root and ♭7th of C7.

Generally speaking, the note selections (which are based on the written melody, not Benson's improvisation) tend to emphasize the ♭3rds of the minor chords, and the 7ths and 3rds of the dominant chords. The root notes are rarely included, as they often stop the forward motion of the melody and are usually provided by the bass anyway.

In measures 14–18, Benson flat out rips through a mess of 16th notes, providing a nice contrast to the mild-mannered melody that he preceded with. In measures 14 and 15, he bases his improvisation on the A Aeolian mode with the addition of the A♯ (♯5th) and E♭ (♭9th) against the D7 chord in measure 15. In measure 16, he blends the G minor pentatonic (with the addition of the 9th) with the C Mixolydian mode over the Gm7 and C7 chords, respectively. Measures 17 and 19 both employ the F Ionian mode over the F6 chord. Measure 18 (C7) finds Benson riffing in the C Mixolydian mode with the addition of the ♯11th (F♯) and ♭9th (D♭) for extra dominant color. In measure 20, he inserts an E7♭9 chord before walking down chromatically from the ♭7th (D), 6th (D♭ or C♯), and ♭6th (C) notes on the way to Am7 in measure 21. Dig that the C functions as the ♭3rd (target note) of Am. In measures 21 and 22, Benson reverts back to the A Aeolian mode, emphasizing the ♭3rd and root over the Am7 chord and ending on the cool ♭7th (D) leading tone of E7.

Performance

As always, finger the octaves on strings 6 and 4, and 5 and 3 with the index and ring fingers, muting the in between string with the side of the index finger if you use a flat pick. If you want to sound exactly like Benson, use your thumb on string 5 and your index finger on string 3 and move them up and down simultaneously from your wrist and forearm.

Fig. 1

Study

After playing "cat and mouse" with organist Clarence Palmer in what almost qualifies as an interlude, Benson comes roaring back in around 2:40. For the next 28 measures, he demonstrates his total mastery of playing through changes as well as over a one or two-chord vamp. He starts out trilling the C ($\flat$3rd of Am7) and the D ($\flat$7th of E7) notes and then applies a repeating triplet figure consisting of E, D, and C over the Am7 and the E7 up to measure 6. Though the triplets are so fast that they operate more as a "sound effect" than deliberate, distinct harmony, the note selection is not capricious. The C note, for instance, is quite consonant with the Am7, but does tweak the ear slightly over the E7 chord where it functions as the $\flat$6th.

In measures 7–10 (E7 = V7), Benson blends the E Mixolydian mode: root (E), 2nd (F$\sharp$), 3rd (G$\sharp$), 4th (A), 5th (B), 6th (C$\sharp$), and $\flat$7th (D), with the F jazz melodic minor scale: $\flat$9th (F), $\flat$3rd (G), 3rd (A$\flat$ or G$\sharp$), $\flat$5th (B$\flat$), $\flat$6th (C), $\flat$7th (D), and root (E). As you can see, the F jazz melodic minor scale provides a passel of hip altered tones ($\flat$3rd, $\flat$5th, $\flat$6th, $\flat$9th) as well as the necessary 3rd, $\flat$7th, and root. The different degrees offered by the E Mixolydian mode are the 2nd (F$\sharp$), 4th (A), 5th (B), and 6th (C$\sharp$). (Note: The F jazz melodic minor shares five out of seven degrees with the A Aeolian mode). In addition, Benson also throws in the major 7th (D$\sharp$). Inasmuch as this section of the solo is a one-chord vamp, the vast selection of notes at his disposal allows him to construct long, melodic lines full of tension and release.

Measures 12–19 consist of a two chord, two-measure vamp of Am7–E7. In measures 12 and 13, Benson sticks to the A Aeolian mode (except for a passing E$\flat$ note) over the Am7 and E7 chords—emphasizing the root (A), $\flat$7th (G), and $\flat$3rd (C) notes over the Am7 and the root (E), $\flat$7th (D), and sus4 (A) notes over the E7. Starting in measure 14, however, he switches from A Aeolian to E Mixolydian, respectively. Breaking up the surplus of single notes, he includes a pair of 6ths (C/E) in measure 12 (Am7) and three descending 3rds (F$\sharp$/D, F/D$\flat$, and E/C, resolving to E) in measure 19.

Measures 20–21 revert back to the E7 vamp as Benson follows suit with the F jazz melodic minor scale and the E Mixolydian mode as in measures 7–10. Notice the harmony in measure 22, where he plays 4ths (B$\flat$/F and D/A) along with a 2nd inversion E$\flat$sus (A$\flat$/E$\flat$/B$\flat$) triple stop for musical tension.

Performance

Besides adhering to a strict regimen of down and up pick strokes, notice that almost every measure can be started with the index finger of the left hand. Those 16th-note triplets are killers at any tempo and can only be executed rapidly and cleanly by slow, methodical practice. Also, play the slippery pull-offs in measures 4–6 with your pinky, ring, and index fingers. At this high of a fret position the stretch should not be too bad, especially on a shorter scale Gibson. Now, if you play a Strat and have smaller than average hands...good luck!

Fig. 2

Solo (2:40 - 3:37)

* played slightly behind the b eat

FIGURE 3

Study

At around 4:19, Benson takes his long, adventuresome solo in a new direction. In measures 1–9, he stays close to the A Aeolian mode, but approaches his note selection and phrasing in a manner dynamically different from his previous musical musings. Measure 2 (Am7) contains two speedy G7 arpeggios that just happen to be constructed from the G, B, D, and F notes from the A Aeolian mode. In measure 3, Benson makes a non-jazzy bend of the F♯ (6th) a half step to G while adding serious blues vibrato. The real surprise starts to appear in measures 5–9 (alternating measure of Am7 and E7) where he sustains and isolates a few notes while applying a heavy, loopy vibrato. The F♯ (rather than the Aeolian F) in measure 5 (Am7) and the F (♭9th) in measure 6 (E7) create an unusual dissonance. After continuing to play sparsely through measures 9 and 10, he sets off on a 16-measure improvisational odyssey through the land of E7. Theoretically, he calls on the same combination of scales (E Mixolydian, F jazz melodic minor, along with the bold major 7ths in measure 11) that he did previously. His phrasing, however, is more dynamic, even in the quicker passages. Though there are few actual rests, the ever-changing combinations of eighth and sixteenth notes, peppered with snappy triplets, gives his long lines a breathless sense of anticipation as he careens between different registers.

Measure 19 is the climactic turning point in the solo as Benson twists the neck of his axe into a pretzel with a string of sixteenth-note triplets. Combined with the "outside" F jazz melodic minor scale, this measure is absolutely riveting. Except for the almost "prestidigitation" 16th note phrase in measure 21 (check out the extreme register leap!) and the slashing 16th notes in measure 22, Benson begins to slowly let the air out of the balloon. In measure 24–28, he returns to the A Aeolian mode and plays a syncopated descending line that resolves to the 5th (E) and root (A) of Am in measure 28. The song form then starts anew with the Am7 chord (not shown) as the organ solo begins.

Performance

The amazing number of rhythmic variations that Benson plays is the result of his broad experience in several classic genres of American music. Without duplicating his exact career (a time-consuming if not impossible task), the only way to learn his phenomenal phrasing is to deliberately play and analyze each measure of these selected passages. Of course, it would not hurt to also listen to his influences— particularly Charlie "Yardbird" Parker and Wes "Thumb" Montgomery.

Fig. 3

Solo (4:19 - 5:08)

* played slightly behind the beat

Low Down and Dirty

(Giblet Gravy, 1968)
By George Benson

While not every great jazz guitarist has the deep blues as their roots (Django Reinhardt, Johnny Smith, Jim Hall, and Pat Metheny come immediately to mind), it adds an immeasurable quantity of "soul" to the music of George Benson, Kenny Burrell, Wes Montgomery, Joe Pass, Barney Kessel, Herb Ellis, and others. On top of that, while many bluesy jazzers can run through the changes on an uptempo number, few are the number who can "get down in the alley" with a slow blues. Along with the aforementioned Kenny Burrell, George Benson, however, would be (and has been) right at home with B.B. King.

"Low Down and Dirty" is an original, slow 12-bar blues that revels in funk. Clocking in at 8:34, it gives Benson the room to stretch his chops and indulge his passion for the foundation of his art. The result is a sumptuous treat for fans of the bend, the slur, and the glissando.

FIGURE 1

Study

In its most basic form, the 12-bar progression reads I–IV–I–I–IV–IV–I–VI–II–V–I–V, all dominant chords. Benson relies almost entirely on the composite B♭ blues scale (blues scale and Mixolydian mode) throughout the head of the tune. Over the I chord (B♭) he emphasizes the 3rd (D) and ♭7th (A♭) notes out of the root position of the composite scale at fret 6 in measures 1, 3, 4, 7, and 8. In measure 2 of the IV chord (E♭), he remains at the same position but focuses on the ♭3rd bent a hip quarter step. This note, in between the ♭3rd and 3rd, is known as the true "blue note." One of the prime lessons to learn when playing the blues is that the ♭3rd of the I chord is the ♭7th of the IV chord.

Like the consummate jazz and blues guitarist that he is, Benson moves out of the tonic scale when it is appropriate. In measures 5 and 6 (IV), he relocates to the E♭ composite scale at fret 11, again emphasizing the 3rd (G) and ♭7th (D♭) notes to nail the tonality of the E♭ dominant chord. Measures 7 and 8 constitute the change from I to VI, which is accomplished chromatically (B♭, A, A♭, and G) through the chords. Though he does not concretely acknowledge each 2-measure change, he does address the B♭9 with the 3rd (D), root (B♭), and ♭7th (A♭), the A13 with the ♭7th (G), the A♭13 with the 6th (F, also seen as the 13th) and root (A♭), and the G7#5 with the funky ♭3rd (B♭) and root (G). In measure 9 (II), Benson shifts briefly to the C blues scale with the root (C), ♭7th (B♭), and 5th (G) notes. In measure 10 (V), he returns to the B♭ scale, but emphasizes the root (F), 9th (G), ♭7th (E♭), and sus4 (B♭) notes of F.

The turnaround in measures 11 and 12 contains I, VI, II, and V chord changes with an alteration (G7♭5) and a tri-tone substitution (B9 for F dominant). Benson plays minimally through this section with the ♭3rd, 3rd, and 5th over the I, and a tasty sixth gliss over the B9 that functions as the 6th and root (A♭/B), and the ♭6th and major 7th (G/B♭). He completes the phrase with the F and B♭ notes as anticipation of the I chord (B♭) in the next chorus.

Performance

Like the bonafide bluesman he is, Benson plays out of "blues boxes" during the head. In keeping with the requisite technique, use your index finger as the take-off point for the various hammer-ons, in addition to performing the quarter-step bend in measure 2 by pulling down.

Fig. 1

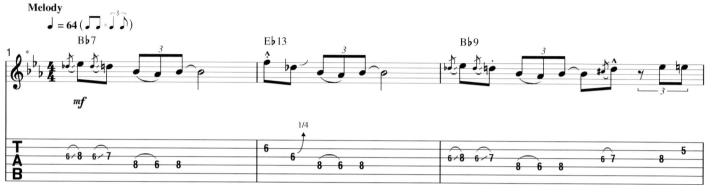

* Key signature denotes Bb Mixolydian.

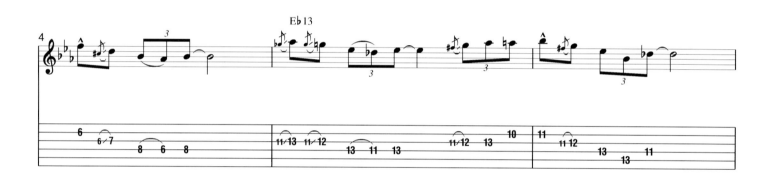

FIGURE 2

Study

In the 2nd chorus of his solo, Benson starts to incorporate more harmony into his single-note improvisation. In measure 1 (I), he employs 6ths from B♭ Mixolydian along with the groovy C♯/E (♯9/♭5th) interval on beat 3. In measure 2 (IV), he changes to the E♭ Mixolydian mode for a series of 6ths that end on D♭/F (♭7th and 9th). Tangy 4ths and 5ths on the top strings appear in measures 2 and 3 (I) that resolve to an interval of a ♭3rd double stop (A♭/F) over the tonic. In measure 4, Benson plays two classic double-stop hammer-ons involving the root as a pedal tone with the 5th and 6th notes, and the 9th as a pedal tone along with the 5th and ♯5th notes. Notice the similar ideas in measures 7 (I) and 8 (VI) with the root up an octave as the pedal tone.

Speaking of classic blues moves, measures 6, 9, 10, and 11 contain F/C♯ at fret 13 with the C♯ bent a "real deal" quarter step. The nature of these scale degrees allows them to be played over any and all blues changes. In measure 10 (V), Benson moves the double stop up a minor 3rd to fret 16 (A♭/E) and then back down to fret 13 in order to punctuate this climactic measure in a 12-bar blues. In measures 5 and 6 (IV), he slithers seductively in wide interval leaps for a wonderful dynamic effect involving the root (E♭), 5th (B♭), and 4th (A♭) notes.

Performance

Scale-wise, Benson continues to work the B♭ composite scale for the most part, though he changes to the E♭ composite scale in measure 5 (IV). Take note, however, that in measures 7-9 he plays in the octave position of the G relative minor scale between frets 15 and 18. This scale is a useful and versatile improvisational tool, especially for the blues, inasmuch as the root, 9th and 13th notes fall comfortably under the fingers. Benson engages in a "call and response" with himself in measures 7 and 8, repeating a 3-note phrase including the 13th, root, and 9th in alternation with the harmony lick previously described in paragraph one.

Benson goes out in style in measure 12 over the V chord with a repeating figure comprised of the ♭3rd (A♭), root (F), and major 7th (E♮), all designed to tease the ear into listening to the next chorus.

Fig. 2

FIGURE 3

Study

Benson's last solo chorus before he returns to the head contains some of his most traditional blues licks and a blast of outrageously fast lines. Though it goes by in the blink of an eye, the pedal tone (root) in measure 1, played against the 4th (Eb), b5th (E), and 5th (F), sets the (blues) stage for what follows. On the last beat of the measure, Benson jumps up to the 11th position to play the 6th, 5th, and b7th. Remaining there momentarily, he shifts his attention to the IV chord and the Eb composite scale before whipping back down to the root position of the Bb composite scale where he emphasizes the 9th (F), b7th (Db), 5th (Bb), and 3rd (G) notes.

In measures 5 and 6, Benson raises the bar for all other blues (and jazz) guitarists as he glides seamlessly through a series of 10- and 8-note groupings from the Bb Mixolydian mode to accentuate the IV chord. He stays at the same position as the Bb9, A13, Ab13, and G7#5 chords (measures 7 and 8) go by, letting the harmonies shift according to the chord change as he basically repeats the same notes in measure 5.

By measure 9 (II), Benson is ready to change keys to the C blues scale where he plays off the C triad on beat I with the 9th (D) and b7th (Bb) notes. On beat 4, he rolls out a descending turnaround pattern in F that resolves on beat 2 of measure 10 (V) with the classic lick of the b3rd (Ab) hammered to the 3rd (A) and ending on the root (F). Not content with this surfeit of harmony, he ventures on in the root position of the Bb composite scale on beats 3 and 4, emphasizing the b7th (Eb), b6th (Db), and root (F) notes. Without pausing, on the third triplet of beat 4 Benson plays the 3rd (D) and root (Bb) notes of measure 11 (I) to begin his stroll through the turnaround. See how he slips into the G relative minor scale at fret 3 on beat 2 before heading back up to the root position of the Bb composite scale on beat 3 with notes that "suggest" the change to G7b5 (root, b7th, b5th). In measure 12, he lands hard on the b3rd (Eb) of C (II) for musical tension before resolving, with blues harmony, to the b7th (Eb) of F.

Performance

Again, the index finger is the prime indicator for most of the licks and phrases. This is especially true for measure 1, where you want to anchor your index finger at fret 6 on string 1 (B♭). This is also critical in measure 4 and 11; a chromatic phrase of C, C♯, D, and E♭ on string 3 absolutely requires the use of the index, middle, ring, and pinky fingers.

About measures 5 and 6: As scary as they look (and sound), upon closer inspection the scales reveal themselves to command basic pentatonic fingerings (index and ring fingers), except for string 2, which contains the ♭7th, 6th, and 5th notes (pinky, ring, and index) from the B♭ Mixolydian mode.

Fig. 3

Solo #2 (Last Chorus)

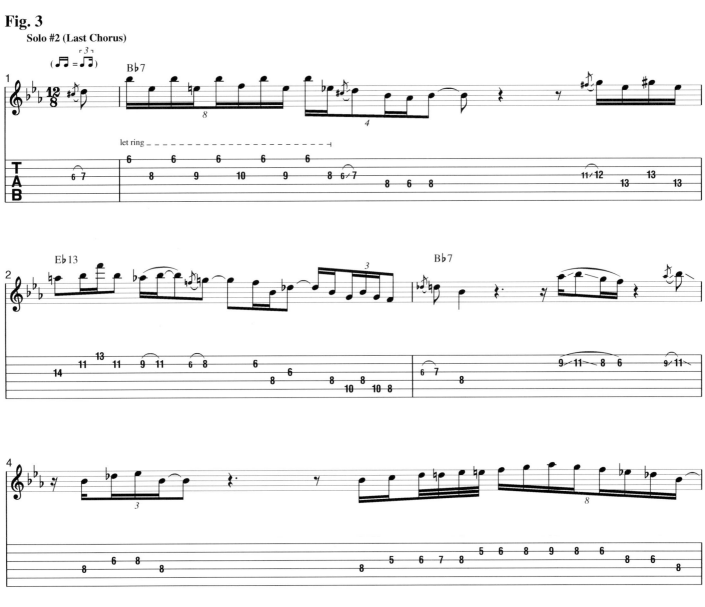

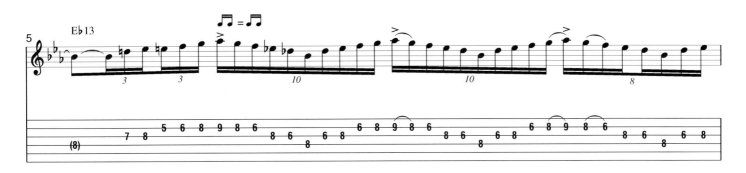

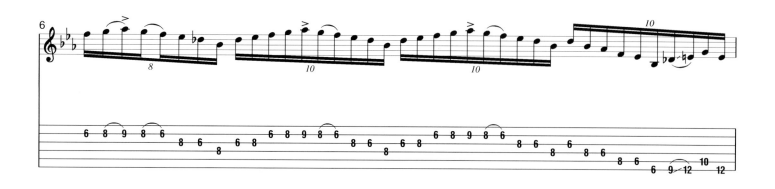

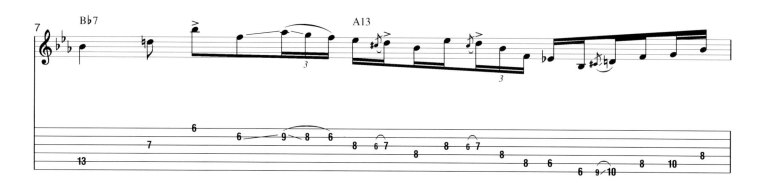

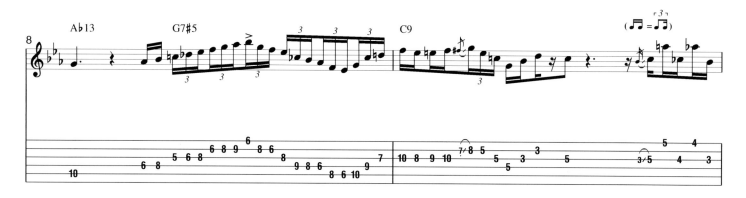

Poquito Spanish, Poquito Funk

(Standing Together, 1998)
By George Benson, Luis Vega and Kenny Gonzalez

Returning to the style of his great commercial triumphs in the late seventies, George Benson played and sang for the "lite jazz" audience with *Standing Together.* Smooth pop melodies predominate, with gentle Latin rhythms, lush keyboards, and polite guitar work supporting.

"Poquito Spanish, Poquito Funk" shows Benson's scat chops to still be one of his appealing assets. His tone is fatter and "woodier" than on some of his earlier recordings, and his expressive touch is still much in evidence.

FIGURE 1

Study

The entire song is constructed upon a two-measure vamp of Am7–D7♭9–Gm7–B♭13. The key signature is C, relative to Am, with Benson using the A Aeolian mode as the basis for his melody and improvisation. The "head" (such as it is) consists of four measures, or twice through the progression. Over this section, Benson plays a melody in octaves while scatting along with his guitar. Notice that the melody is actually two nine-note phrases that are alike except for the last two notes. In the first phrase, Benson plays the following notes (in octaves), notated relative to the chords:

Am7: B (9th), E (5th), B, B♭ (♭9th)
D7♭9: E♭ (♭9th), Bb (♭6th)
Gm7: A (9th)
B♭13: D (3rd)

In the second phrase, he substitutes the following notes:

Gm7: B♭ (♭3rd) in place of A.
B♭13: G (6th) in place of D.

The lack of root notes and the preponderance of 9ths and ♭9ths add a buoyant musical tension perfectly in keeping with the lilting, dreamy nature of the piece. In measure 9, Benson begins improvising variations on the melody. By measures 13 and 14 he starts digging in to the harmony by playing G (♭7th) and C (♭3rd) over the Am7, C (♭7th) over D7♭9, F (♭7th) and D (5th) over Gm7, and C (9th) and B♭ (root) over B♭13.

On beat 4 (B♭13) in measure 20, Benson switches from octaves to a 5th (F/B♭), repeating it in measures 21 and 22 over the Am7 (♭6th and ♭9th), D7♭9 (♭6th and ♭3rd), and Gm7 (♭7th and ♭3rd). He finishes the increment by emphasizing the G (6th) note over the B♭13 chord. As he does so often, Benson plays many altered notes to create and maintain musical tension. In measures 23 and 24, he continues the single-note line begun in measure 22 and walks up in stages through B♭, C, C♯ (functioning as the major 7th—leading tone—of D), D, and G before climaxing on F (♭7th of G) bent one-half step to the major 7th (F♯). Benson remains in the root position (around fret 5) of the A Aeolian mode for the remainder of the measure, bending the C (4th of G) up one-half step to D♭ (♭5th) and then playing B♭ (root), C (9th), D (3rd), and G (6th) over the B♭13 chord to suggest resolution.

In measures 25 and 26 (except for the rest on beats 3 and 4 of the B♭13 chord), Benson employs the G note on string 2 as a pedal tone, under which he adds the lower octave and B♭ on string 4. In addition, he also sneaks in the C on string 3 (creating a 5th). On top of that, he also adds the F on string 5. Be sure to see that the octave is the overriding sound with the other notes providing additional harmony. Though short, this is a beautiful section. Here is how the harmony is analyzed:

Am7: G (♭7th), B♭ (♭9th), C (♭3rd)
D7♭9: G (4th), F (♭3rd), B♭ (♭6th)
Gm7: G (root), F (♭7th), C (4th)

"Poquito Spanish, Poquito Funk" involves harmonic changes, but due to the rapidity of their repetition, the overall effect is of a modal progression. Therefore, after Benson establishes the chord changes with his melody and initial improvisation, he gets further and further away from the strict structure and begins to play to the Am7 tonality.

Performance

Benson's standard fingerings for octaves apply throughout. Bend the F and C notes in measure 24 with the index finger by pulling down. The pattern in measures 25 and 26 should be approached as such: Index finger on low G, pinky on high G, ring finger for B♭, index finger (as a barre) for C, and the middle finger for the F. The high C in measure 26 can be accessed by flattening the pinky to form a small barre.

Fig. 1

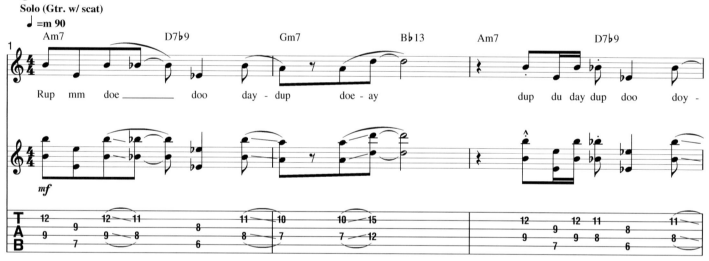

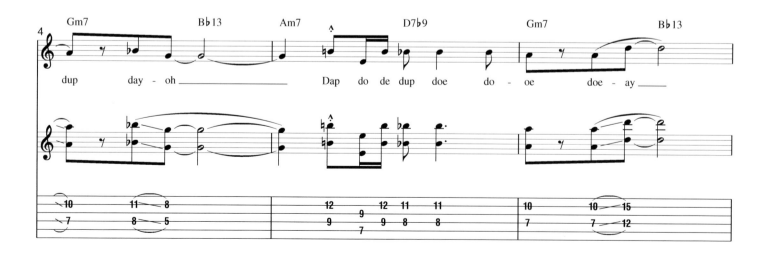

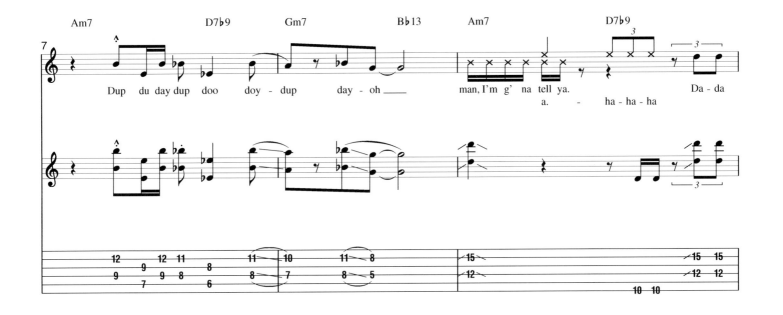

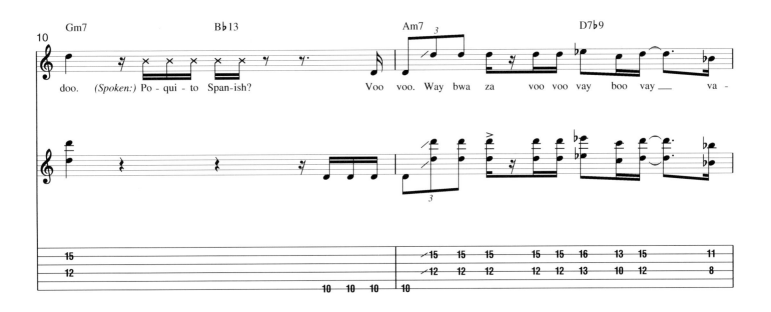

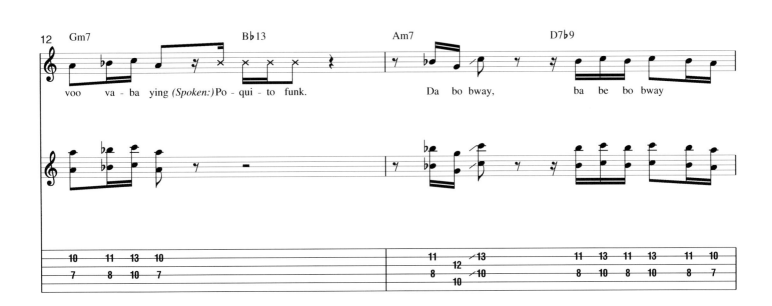

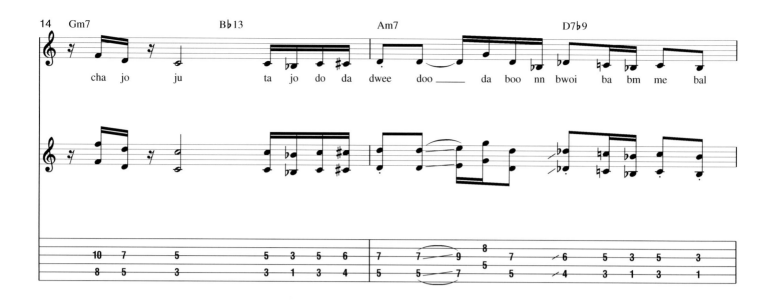

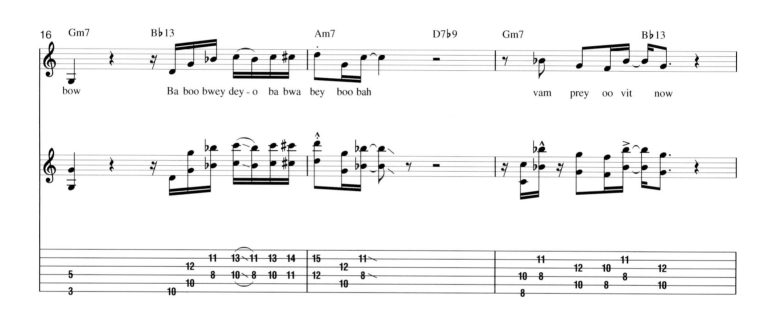

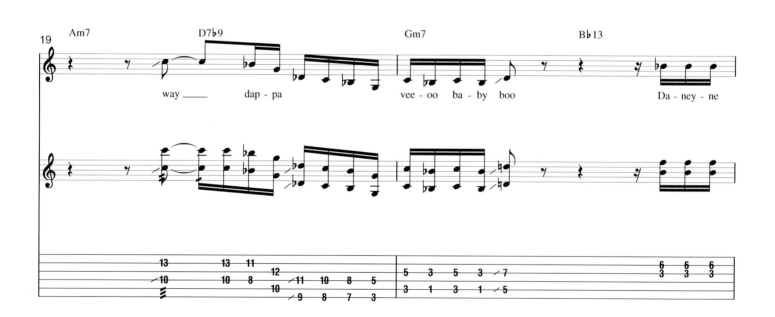

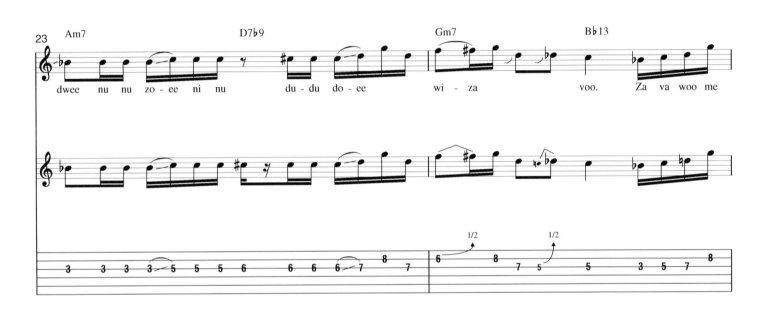

Sack Of Woe

(Giblet Gravy, 1968)

By Julian Adderley

Written by Julian "Cannonball" Adderly, "Sack Of Woe" is a finger-snappin' 12-bar blues with a decidedly soulful head appropriate to the sixties era from which it sprang. Alto saxist Adderly gravitated towards a successful career in the sixties playing R&B-flavored jazz after having previously served with Miles Davis among others. His "Mercy, Mercy, Mercy" (actually written by keyboardist Joe Zawinul) was a crossover hit and proved the viability of top notch jazz musicians "getting down."

George Benson pays more homage to his roots on this blues than he does on most. Part of the reason is that the fundamental progression contains straight I–IV–V changes. Another is the spirit of the basic "boogaloo" head spills over into his solos. The combination results in some of the most funky riffs he ever committed to *vinyl*. (Ah, those were the days!)

FIGURE 1

(Note: All 4 Figures contain repetitive tension licks that tend to resolve to the tonic chord in the last measure of each chorus)

Study

The head consists of a 12-bar "verse" and a 14-measure "bridge" in the key of F Dorian. The verse has Benson playing a two-measure lick three times during the 12 measures, which is a time-honored tradition in the blues and swing jazz for building a memorable head. The notes C, E♭, B♭, A♭, F, and E♭ are derived from the F blues scale. Here is how they relate to the three chord changes:

I (F7): C (5th), E♭ (♭7th), B♭ (4th), A♭ (♭3rd), F (root)
IV (B♭7): C (9th), E♭ (4th), B♭ (root), A♭ (♭7th), F (5th)
V (C7): C (root), E♭ (♭3rd), B♭ (♭7th), A♭ (♭6th), F (4th)

Notice how this particular selection of notes relates with blues harmony to each of the chord changes. In the bridge, a similar concept is at work. 3rds, 4ths, and a run down the F blues scale combine in a four-measure phrase to elucidate the changes. Note, however, that the 3rds for the I and V changes are loosely derived from the F Mixolydian mode, and the ones for the IV chord are based on the B♭ Mixolydian mode (Note: A/F functions as the 6th and 4th of C in measure 21). The 4ths (F/C and E/B—open strings) and the 3rds (C/A♭) in measures 13, 14, 18, and 22 relate to both the I and IV chords like this:

I (F7): F/C (root and 5th), C/A♭ (5th and ♭3rd), E/B (major 7th and ♭5th)
IV (B♭7): F/C (5th and 9th), C/A♭ (9th and ♭7th), E/B (♭5th and ♭9th)

The run is similar to the one in the verse.

Performance

Play the 3rds in measures 13 and 21 with your middle and index fingers, and the ones in measure 17 with your ring and index fingers. The 4th and 3rd double stops in measures 14, 18, and 22 are best played by barring with the index finger.

Fig. 1

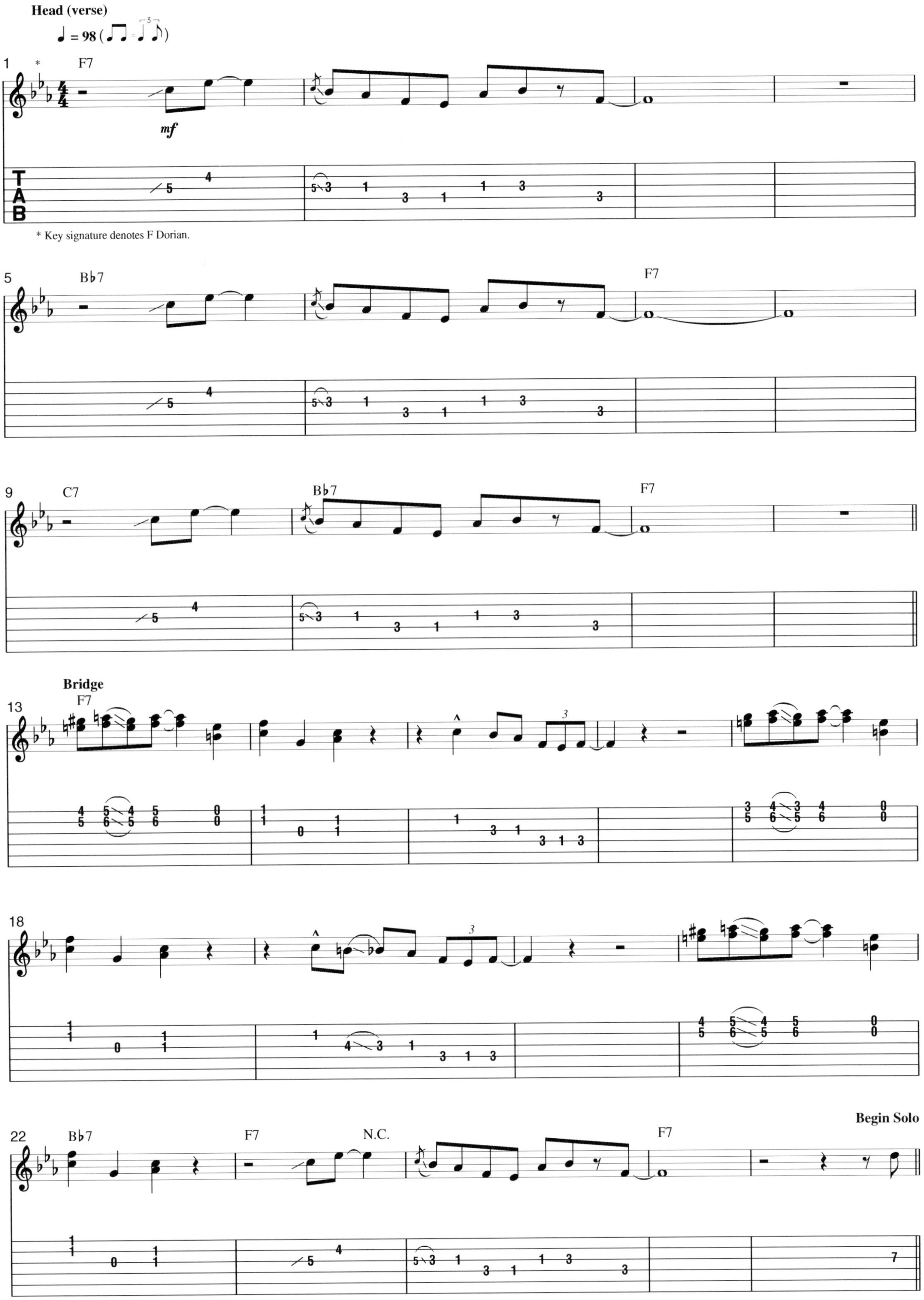
Head (verse)
♩ = 98
F7
mf
T
A
B
* Key signature denotes F Dorian.
B♭7
F7
C7
B♭7
F7
Bridge
F7
B♭7
F7
N.C.
F7
Begin Solo

FIGURE 2

Study

The 1st solo chorus shows Benson bopping along, popping and comping as he chooses choice "blues" notes over the changes. With the F composite blues scale as his palette, he emphasizes the root (F), 9th (G), 6th (D), 3rd (A), 5th (C), 4th (B♭), and ♭3rd (A♭) bent a tasty quarter step over the I (F7) chord in measures 2, 3, 4, 5, 8, and 9. Over the IV (B♭7) chord in measures 7 and 11, the D, G, A♭, and F notes function as the 3rd, 6th, ♭7th, and 5th in the key of B♭. Check out how Benson plays roughly the same notes in measures 9–11 to suavely harmonize with the I, V, and IV chords. The analysis goes like this:

I (F7): F (root), D (6th)
V (C7): F (4th), D (9th)
IV (B♭7): F (5th), D (3rd)

The quarter-note bends are purely ornamental, but add a nice "organic" touch. Just as important as the single-note lines, however, are the well-placed comp chords. Dig how Benson slides down organically one half step above from G♭9♯5 to F9 in measures 2, 4, and 12. Likewise, appreciate the cool move from B♭13 to B♭7 in measure 6.

Performance

Always try to anticipate the chords following the licks by ending on the proper finger. In measure 2, end on the F note on string 2 with the index finger in order to quickly shift it to the B♭ note on string 4 for the G♭9♯5 chord. In measure 4, end on the F note at fret 10 with the ring finger. In measure 6, form the double stop (after finishing on the sustained F note with the index finger) with the index and ring fingers, adding the G note on string 2 with the pinky. Then, slide the index and ring fingers down one fret for the implied B♭13 chord on beat 2. Lift the pinky and replace it with the middle finger on beat 4 to form the implied B♭7 chord.

Fig. 2

FIGURE 3

Study

The 6th solo chorus shows Benson repeating a hypnotic triplet lick for 10 measures (counting measure 12 from the previous chorus as a pickup). As in Figures 1 and 2, the F note(s) is carefully selected to harmonize idiomatically with the I, IV, and V chords. In this case, with the F being the root note of the key, it would be hard to go wrong. Nonetheless, it is instructional to look at the changing harmonies, as simple as they may be (Note: Though the F notes are in the same octave, the fact that they are on different strings and that Benson has to shift quickly from one to the other gives the lick a sound unique from the repetition of just one note):

I (F7): F (root)
IV (B♭7): F (5th)
V (C7): F (4th)

In measure 11 (IV), Benson repeats the F notes again before playing a piquant blues double stop (C/A♭)—repeated in measure 12 (I)—that functions as the 9th and ♭7th, and 5th and ♭3rd of B♭7 and F7, respectively. The B♭7 chord is further embellished with C and E♭ (9th and 4th) notes while the F7 also contains the root (F) and D (6th) notes. Measure 13 (I) has a horn-like accent provided by E♭/C♭ (B) that acts as the ♭7th and ♭5th notes.

Performance
Play the repeating F notes with the pinky and index fingers, low to high. Play the double stops in measures 11 and 12 with the middle and index fingers. Smear the quarter-step double-stop bends in measure 13 with the ring finger by pulling down.

Fig. 3

FIGURE 4

Study

Solo chorus number 7 also uses a considerable amount of repetition to create delicious and bluesy musical tension. In measures 2–5 (I) Benson promotes F/C (root and 5th) as the defining harmony of a 4th. He mainly rests (whew!) in measures 6 and 7 of the IV chord before changing tactics in measures 8 and 9 (I) and 10 (V). Over the I chord he plays A♭/C (♭3rd and 5th) and F/B♭ (root and 4th) with the addition of E♭/A♭ (♭7th and ♭3rd) on beat 3 of measure 9 as anticipation into measure 10 (V). There, he repeats E♭/A♭ where it functions as the garlicky ♭3rd and ♭6th before sliding down to D♭/G♭ (♭9th and ♭5th) and resolving (as much by gravity as harmony) to C/F (root and 4th). In measure 11 (IV), Benson proffers a slick, sliding triple stop implying a gnarly B♭6sus to B♭maj9. The double stops on beats 3 and 4 are just smaller versions of the same harmony. Benson gives a virtuoso chord performance in measures 12 and 13 (I) by playing an F13/E♭ inversion, an implied D9th (VI), followed by G♭9 (♭II) and F9 (I).

Performance

Play F/C in measures 2–5 at fret 18 with the (unorthodox) ring and pinky fingers so that you can reach down to fret 15 on string 3 with the index or middle finger where necessary. The reason for this (again) unorthodox fingering can be seen by the bend (with the middle finger) and pull-off (to the index finger) on beat 3 of measure 5.

Play the chords in measure 11 with the middle, index, and pinky fingers, low to high. In measure 12, play the F13/E♭ with the index, ring, pinky, and middle fingers. Play the D9 with the middle, index and ring fingers, and the 9th chords with the index and ring (as a barre) fingers.

Fig. 4

Solo (7th chorus)

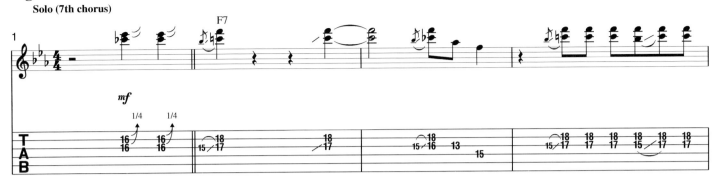

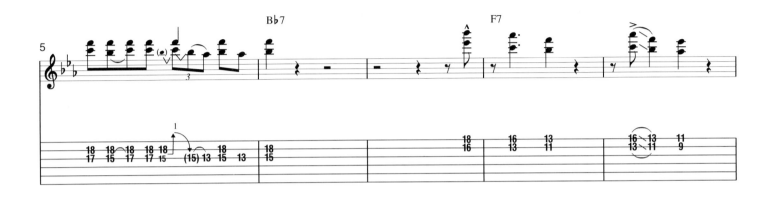

So What
(Beyond the Blue Horizon, 1979)
By Miles Davis

In direct contrast to the "easy listening" jazz of "The Gentle Rain" from *Beyond the Blue Horizon,* "So What" gave George Benson and crew the chance to really "blow" on a great standard. Originally released on Miles Davis's classic milestone *Kind of Blue* in 1959, Benson's version reflected its contemporary setting while acknowledging the enormous influence of soloists John Coltrane, Julian "Cannonball" Adderly, and Davis himself.

"So What" was recorded during the hey day of jazz-rock fusion and contains tempo and rhythmic changes popular in the genre. Its basic modal structure (the songs on *Kind of Blue* were all written around a specific mode) was attractive to musicians like Benson who were raised on blues, rock, and jazz. Of course, he was so adept at running changes, even at bebop tempos, that the two key modulations must have seemed like a stroll in the park.

FIGURE 1

Study

The 32-measure song form consists of 16 measures of Dm7, 8 measures of E♭m7, and 8 measures of Dm7. Based on the D and E♭ Dorian modes to complement the minor 7 chords, the incremental phrase is 8 measures long and is constructed from three different two-measure riffs. The first riff (measures 1 and 2) contains the 5th (A), 6th (B), ♭7th (C), root (D), and 2nd (E). The second riff (measures 3 and 4) contains the same notes with the addition of the 5th after the last root note. At this point, the first riff repeats in measures 5 and 6. Following is the third variation (measures 7 and 8) which consists of the 2nd, root, and 5th. The second 8-measure increment is virtually the same.

Starting in measure 17, the key modulates up one half step to E♭ minor and all the riffs from the first 8 measures (Dm7) move up the neck accordingly. In measure 25, the key modulates back down one half step to D minor and repeats the first 8 measures once again.

Note that in the original Miles Davis version bassist Paul Chambers plays the head unaccompanied. Here, Benson plays the head with bassist Ron Carter accompanying him, though not in note-for-note unison.

Performance

Begin each two-measure riff on the 5th with the pinky finger and end on each root with the pinky. In the alternate riffs where the phrase ends on the 5th, use the ring finger.

Fig. 1

* Key signature denotes D Dorian.

FIGURE 2

Study

In his second solo chorus, Benson works mostly out of the Dorian mode, but also shifts to the Aeolian mode by flatting the 6th (B♭ in D minor and C in E♭ minor) as both scales "fit" within this modal tune. In addition, he also occasionally inserts the ♭9th (E♭ in D minor and E in E♭ minor) for extra "color." Be aware that, due to the static nature of the chord changes, almost all dynamics and melodic interest must come from Benson's note selection and particularly, his phrasing. Looking at his solo from that perspective, several concepts are revealed. Number one, he composes his solo in roughly four-measure phrases that usually peak (highest note) once in one of the four measures. Number two, this peak usually occurs around the 5th, which is often repeated over the course of two beats, serving as a kind of resolution for all the musical tension generated around it. Number three, Benson brackets his undulating eighth-note forays with quarter notes and rests within the first four measures (and a nice, bluesy quarter-step bend on the 5th in measure 2) and the last eight measures.

Another dynamic effect employed by Benson is his method of responding to the two modulations. When the tonality moves up to E♭ minor in measure 17, he sustains (briefly) the tart ♭5th (A) and rests for a measure and a half, drawing extra attention to the key change. Then, when the key modulates back to D minor in measure 25, he reverses the process, resting first for a half measure and then hanging a ♭6th (B♭) out for our appreciation. This is followed by a leisurely "walk" with regular rests down a "D scale" with the ♭9th (E♭), major 7th (D♭) and major 3rd (F♯(G♭)—Yeow!) before unambiguously settling back in to the D Dorian mode.

Benson is known for including chords or chord forms in his single-note improvisations. Though on the surface he seems to be foregoing that approach in this chorus, close examination reveals a Dm arpeggio in measure 7 and an E♭m arpeggio in measure 24.

Performance

Measures 4, 6, 19, and 24 should begin with the pinky. Aside from that, notice that his playing tends to be quite "vertical" (a Benson trademark) in most measures. Adjust your fingerings accordingly so that you can be in position, as much as possible, to grab notes within a 4- or 5-fret stretch without moving your hand.

Fig. 2

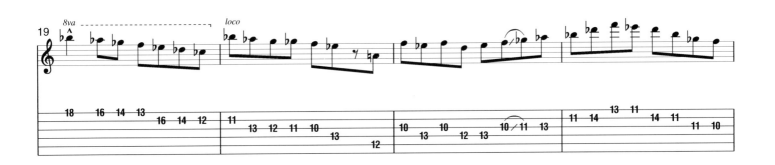

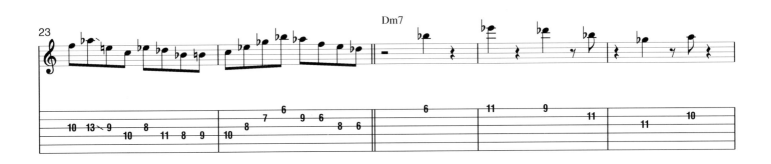

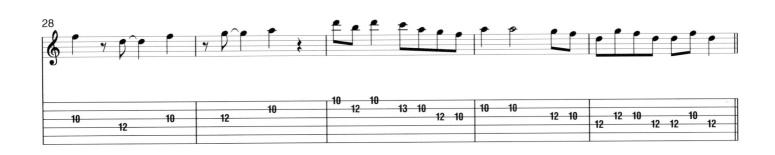

Song for My Father

(Goodies, 1968)

By Horace Silver

"Song for My Father" is a soulful classic from pianist Horace Silver that has been covered many times by many types of musicians. Its gentle, yet insistent groove and melancholy melody is especially enticing to jazzers with a strong R&B bent like George Benson, or R&B folks with jazz leanings like Jimmy McGriff. Fans of quality pop music will recognize the intro bass figure as being respectfully lifted for the hook of Steely Dan's "Rikki Don't Lose that Number."

Like its sister album *Giblet Gravy* from the same year, *Goodies* presented a wide and tasty selection of contemporary radio fare and original blues along with accessible jazz. The passage of time and Benson's mega-success that followed almost a decade later has not diminished the winning combination of great tunes, advanced harmony, and funky R&B attitude contained in these tracks.

FIGURE 1

Study

"Song for My Father" follows an AAB arrangement with each section eight measures in length. In the key of Fm, it uses a handful of bluesy dominant chords derived from the F Aeolian mode:

Section A

Fm (i): two measures, E♭7 (♭VII7): two measures, D♭7 (♭VI7): one measure, C7 (V7): one measure, and Fm: two measures.

Section B

E♭9: two measures, Fm9: two measures, E♭9 and D♭9: one measure, C9: one measure, and Fm: two measures.

Benson harmonizes the melody with chords and double stops interspersed with judiciously placed single notes from the F Aeolian mode. As with most chord melody arrangements, the top note of the chord is almost always part of the melody. True to his roots (once again), he is not afraid to mix common R&B voicings like the E♭7 in measures 4 and 5, and the C7 in measure 7 with a hip C7♯5, also in measure 7. And, where another jazz guitarist might overwhelm the simple beauty of the melody with too many "outside" harmonies, Benson enhances the composition with consonant, diatonic sequences like the pickup measure that leads smoothly to the Fm on beat 1 of measure 2.

In the bridge, Benson chooses more double stops than chords to convey the appropriate harmony. These voicings on strings 3 and 2 complement the horns, blending in as if a natural part of the horn section. And, except for measure 16, he plays abbreviated triple stops for the minor and dominant chords.

Performance

"Song for My Father" has a subtle syncopation despite the direction "even eighths" above the staff. Try to keep your pick hand light and nimble without ignoring the dynamic accents. As with all chord-melody arrangements or those where comp chords are combined with single-note lines, logical fingerings are a strict requirement. For the most part, if you get the single notes right, the chords will fall under your fingers. In measure 2, play the B♭ with the index and the A♭ (on string 2) with the pinky finger. Play the A♭ (on string 1) with the index and the F with the ring finger. In measure 3, play the F with the ring and the E♭ with the index finger. Play the E♭ again with the index finger and the C with the middle finger. In measure 15, play the E♭ with the ring, the D♭ with the index, and the F with the pinky finger. Then, play the D♭ (on string 5) with the index, the A♭ with the ring, the C♭ (B) with the index, and the F with the ring finger. In measures 17 and 18, play the C with the index, the A♭ with the middle, and the F with the ring finger.

Lastly, be sure to use small barres with either the index or ring fingers wherever two notes on consecutive strings are on the same fret.

Fig. 1

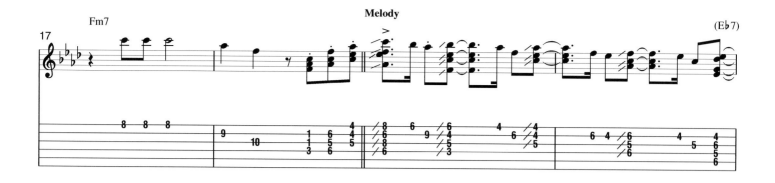

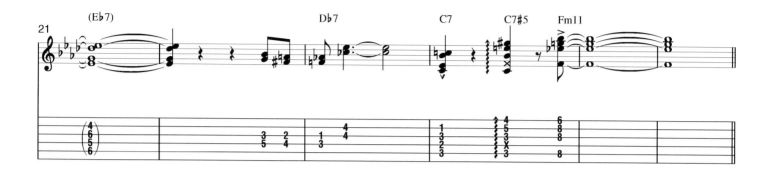

FIGURE 2

Study

Benson's first solo through the song form is a virtuosic lesson in note selection, not to mention phrasing. Using a combination of the F Aeolian and F Dorian modes, he seamlessly runs the changes, artfully delineating the choice notes for each chord. Over the Fm7 chord (measures 1, 2, 7, 8, 9, 10, 15, 16, 19, 20, 23, 24, and 31, with 32 a measure of rest), he leans on the triadic tones: F (root), A♭ (♭3rd), and C (5th). Also highlighted are the E♭ (♭7th), the B♭ (4th), and E (major 7th) as tension notes. Check out how Benson emphasizes the G (9th) in measures 19 and 20 of Fm9.

Over the E♭7 chord (measures 3, 4, 11, 12, 17, 18, 21, and 27), he again covers the chord tones: E♭ (root), G (♭3rd), B♭ (5th), and D♭ (♭7th). In addition, Benson inserts the F (9th) regularly over the E♭7 and the E♭9 chords. For "spice" he also includes the C (6th) and E (♭9th) notes.

For D♭7 (measures 5, 13, 21, and 29), he promotes the chordal indicators D♭ (root), F (3rd), A♭ (5th), and C♭ (♭7th). The E♭ (9th) also makes several appearances to extend the harmony. The C7 (measures 6, 14, 22, and 30) merits the triadic tones: C (root), E (3rd), and G (5th) along with the B♭ (♭7th). The D (9th), D♭ (♭9th), A♭ (♭6th), and G♭ (♭5th) add considerable vibrant color to the V7 chord.

Performance

Like the chord melody section in Figure 1, many of the runs should begin with the pinky or ring fingers. Aside from that, once again Benson often plays vertically and very contained, almost within a "box." Also, dig the bluesy lick in measure 24 where Benson holds down the root (F) at fret 13 with his pinky while adding the B♭, B, and C notes as harmony with his index, middle, and ring fingers, respectively. This whole measure is a trip, requiring efficient, logical fingering to pull it off (no pun intended!) at this tempo. Be sure to play the C note on beat 3 with the pinky, flattening it out across the F that follows. In addition, play the double-string, quarter-step bend in measure 25 (C/A♭) with the ring finger.

Fig. 2

This Masquerade

(Breezin', 1976)
Words and Music by Leon Russell

This is the song that launched a thousand club bands and brought George Benson's outstanding talents as a guitarist and singer together for a historic occasion. A moody, melodramatic minor key ballad with a memorable melody line that finds Benson sounding similar to Stevie Wonder, "This Masquerade" contains a long scat solo.

FIGURE 1

Study

In the key of F minor, this pop classic has a 36-measure solo built on a i–IV7 (Fm–B♭7) vamp. I–IV changes are rooted in the blues and are the perfect two chords to employ in this fashion due to I–IV being the chord change with the most forward harmonic motion. Likewise, moving in reverse IV–I (B♭–F) in the key of F actually implies I–V (B♭–F) in the key of B♭. In other words, a I–IV vamp is totally self-contained and can be repeated endlessly.

Benson takes the F Dorian mode as his scale of choice and weaves a satin tapestry with his voice and guitar. In a two-measure vamp solo of this duration, it is usually not advisable to shift the tonal center from the I to the IV chord in every measure, and Benson follows suit. However, he does deliberately indicate the changes often along his instrumental journey. In measure 2 (i), he plays a simple root (F) and 9th(G) lick that sustains the root, while emphasizing the root (B♭) and ♭7th (A♭) in measure 3 (IV7).

Similar to the one-chord vamp in "So What," soloing over a two-chord vamp requires different improvisational skills than playing over changes like on "Song for My Father." Dynamics of register, texture, note selection, and the use of rests all contribute to making a substantial musical statement. Up through measure 19, Benson does not play any pair of measures in the same scale position except for 4 and 5. For musical texture, in measures 24 and 25 he plays full chords, and in measures 34–37 he purveys double stops in 3rds that harmonize with the changes: E♭/C (♭7th and 5th) over Fm7, and D/B♭ (3rd and root) and C/A♭ (9th and ♭7th) over B♭7 in measures 34 and 35. In measure 36, he plays a series of double stops relative to F Dorian and in measure 37 a series relative to B♭ Mixolydian.

One of the secrets of Benson's note selection process is the care he puts into choosing the highest emphasized note in each measure. In the Fm measures, they are (in order of appearance) G (9th), A♭ (♭3rd), A♭, A♭, B♭ (4th), B♭, C (5th), C, G, F (root), C, C, A♭, A♭, A♭, C, E♭ (♭7th), and B♭. You can see that the A♭ (♭3rd) is the most prominent and is the defining tonality of the Fm7 chord. In the B♭7 measures, they are E♭ (4th), F (5th), C (9th), G (6th), G, C, B♭ (root), B♭, A♭ (♭7th), F, C, F, A♭, C♭ (♭9th), A♭, D (3rd), and F. Notice that the dominant tonality notes of G (6th or 13th) and Ab (♭7th) lead the way to complement the B♭7 chord. Benson also paces his solo in undulating waves with several measures of fewer notes (with rests) contrasted with several measures of a greater concentration, or clusters, of notes.

Performance

You will find that blues scale-type fingerings work in many instances throughout the solo, inasmuch as the F Aeolian/Dorian modes are quite similar to the blues scale in their root and extended positions. In measure 29, play the repeating patterns with the pinky, ring, index, and ring fingers, picking only the first and last note in each grouping.

Fig. 1

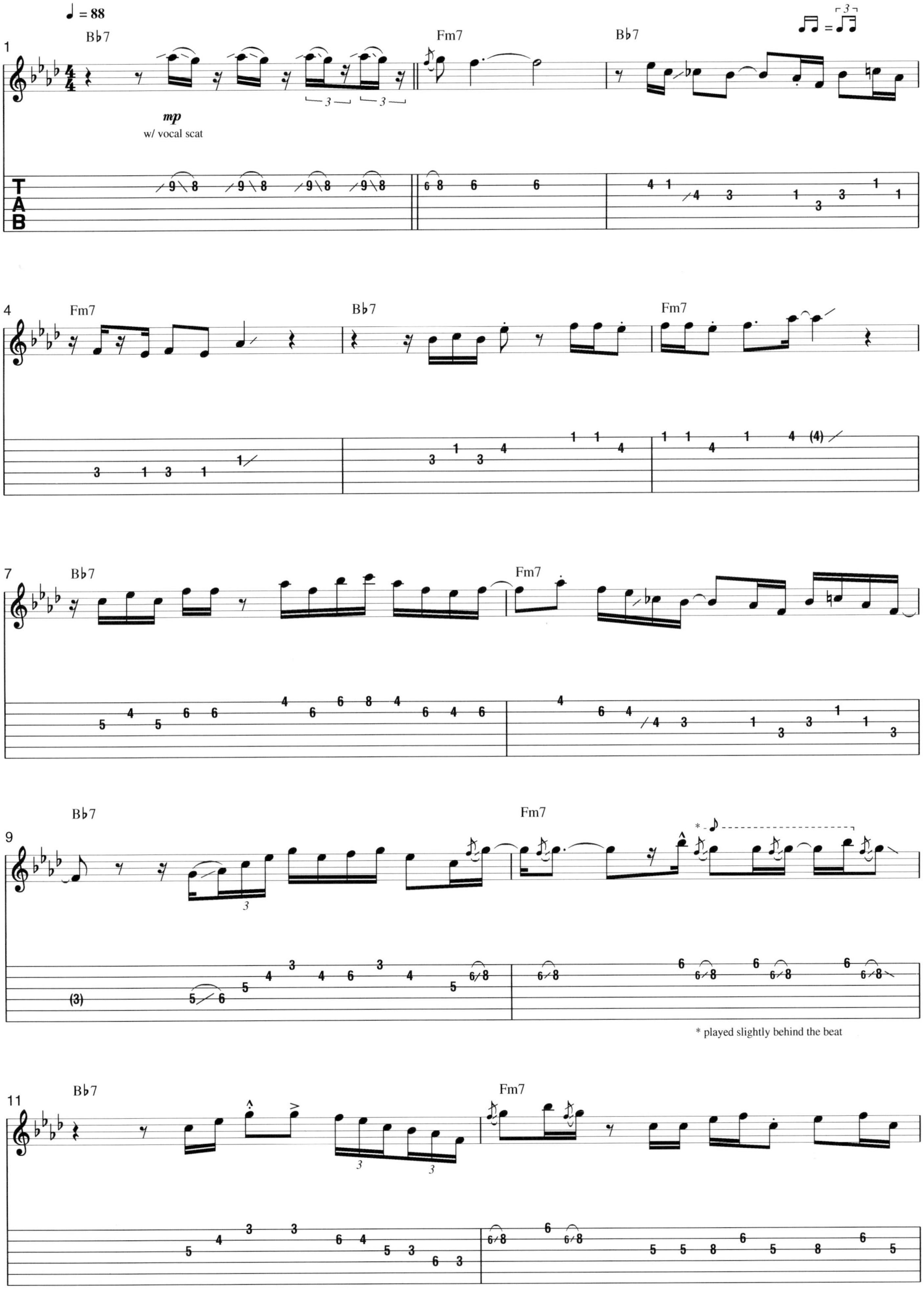

* played slightly behind the beat

What's New?

(Giblet Gravy, 1968)

Words by Johnny Burke
Music by Bob Haggart

This swing-era ballad has been covered by jazz instrumentalists like Milt Jackson and Maynard Ferguson, as well as crooners such as Frank Sinatra. As he does on "Easy Living," George Benson brings his interpretive skills as a singer to bear on his guitar playing on another beautiful melody.

FIGURE 1

Study

As usual for this type of tune, "What's New?" follows the 32-measure AABA form and is in the key of C major. The "A" section is constructed from two four-measure phrases that alternate to make a standard 16-measure section. Check out that measures 2 and 3 contain a cycle of 4ths (B♭–E♭–A♭), as do measures 4 and 5 (D–G–C: II–V–I in the key of C).

A Section

C (I): one measure, B♭m–E♭ (♭vii and ♭iii): one measure, A♭ (♭VI): one measure, Dm–G7 (ii and V7): one measure.

Cm–Am (i and vi): one measure, Dm–G7 (ii and V7): one measure, C–Am (I and vi): one measure, Dm–G7 (ii and V7): one measure. Both four-measure phrases repeat with little variation.

The bridge, or B section, is eight measures in length. Note that the harmonic analysis is seen in terms of a key change to F, although in reality, the key signature is still C.

B Section

F (I): one measure, E♭m–A♭ (♭vii and ♭III): one measure, D♭ (♭VI): one measure, Gm–C7 (ii and V7): one measure, Fm–Dm (i and vi): one measure, Gm–C7 (ii and V7): one measure, Fm (i): one measure, Dm–G7 (vi and II7): one measure.

Benson plays gorgeous chord melody in measures 1–8. His choice of voicings is nothing less than perfect and is a first class primer in the art of the solo guitar, despite the presence of a rhythm section on the track. In measures 2 and 3, he gives a lesson in voice leading as the A♭ note following the B♭m9 chord "leads" to the E♭7 with G on top, G♭ melody note, B♭m7 with F on top, E♭7♭9 with E (♭9th) on top, and resolving to A♭maj7 with E♭ on top. In measure 5, Benson maintains a G common tone on string 2 (after the C note for Cm7 on beat 1) as a descending line on the bottom (string 4) highlights the ♭7th (B♭) of C, the root (A) and major 7th (A♭ or G♯), as a passing tone, and ♭7th (G) of Am7♭5, the 3rd (G♭ or F♯) of Dm7♭5 as a passing tone in measure 6 on the way to F (♭7th) of G7♯5. In measure 8, he performs a similar maneuver as he plays a not quite chromatic line (from C to F, without the E♭) on string 1 while interjecting two cool voicings of G7♭9.

Starting in measure 10, Benson begins playing the changes, with the appropriate scale, on through to measure 32. He groups B♭m9, E♭7, and A♭maj7 into the B♭ minor tonal center, in measures 10 and 11, and uses the B♭ Aeolian mode to hit the 9th (C), root (B♭), and ♭7th (A) of B♭m, the 3rd (G), ♭3rd (G♭), 9th (F), and root (E♭) of E♭7, and the 5th (E♭), 6th (F), 3rd (C), 4th (D♭), major 7th (G), and root (A♭) of A♭maj7. Measure 12 presents a very different picture as Benson approaches Dm7♭5 (half-diminished) obliquely with the root (D) packed in with the ♭9th (E♭) and the major 7th (C♯). The G7, meanwhile, is acknowledged with the "outside" ♭3rd (B♭), sassy ♭9th (A♭), and "inside" 3rd. Measures 13 and 14 (Cm7–Am7♭5–Dm7♭5–G7♯5) are covered with the C minor pentatonic add9 scale emphasizing the 5th (G) and ♭3rd (E♭) over Cm7, a triple stop with the major 7th (A♭), 11th (D), and ♭7th (G) over Am7♭5 followed by a chromatic double-stop sequence of D/A♭ and C♯/G ending on C/G♭ (♭7th and major 3rd) over Dm7♭5. The root (G), ♭7th (F), root (G), and ♯5th (D♯) makes for a convincing resolution over the G7♯5 (V chord).

With few exceptions, Benson improvises over the entire eight-measure bridge with the C Aeolian mode. Each chord change includes one or more prime notes carefully plucked (pun intended!) from the C scale. In measure 17 (F6), they are the root (F), 5th (C), and 6th (D). In measure 18 (A♭7 with a rest on the E♭m9), it's the 5th (E♭). The D♭maj7 in measure 19 gets an embarrassment of riches with the major 7th (C), root (D♭), 5th (A♭), and 3rd (F). The Gm7♭5 and C7♯9 chords in measure 20 receive the ♭3rd (B♭) and root (G), and the 5th (G) and ♯9th (E♭), respectively. In measure 21, the Fm7 is neatly nailed by the ♭3rd (A♭), which also serves as the ♭5th of Dm7♭5.

The last A section adheres fairly close to the scale choices used in measures 9–16. An exception occurs in measure 29 (Cm7 and Am7♭5), however, when Benson plays descending arpeggios over the Cm7 (5th, ♭3rd, and root) and B♭ passing chord (5th, 3rd and root), with an "outside" selection of notes over the Am7♭5 (♭6th (F) and major 3rd (D♭)) that ends "inside" on the ♭7th (G). See that in measure 30 Benson continues the concept with the ♭9th (E♭), ♭7th (C), and ♭5th (A♭) notes of Dm7♭5, walking down chromatically to the 4th (G) and dissonant major 3rd (F♯), and maintaining the tension with the 5th (D), ♭6th (E♭), ♭3rd (B♭), and ♭9th (A♭) of G7♯5 before reaching consonance and resolution in measures 31 and 32 (C6).

Performance

Like "Easy Living," it is important to have a fingering system for the chord melody in measures 1–8. In measure 2, for instance, play the A♭ note on string 2 with the pinky and then move that down one fret to access the G note of the E♭7 chord. Then use the middle finger for the G♭ note on string 2, shifting to the index finger for the barre at fret 6 (B♭m7), while adding the thumb for the low B♭ note on string 6. Another instructional example would be measure 5. Play the G on string 2 with the ring finger, followed by the B♭ and A notes on string 4 with the index finger. Next, barre strings 3 and 2 with the ring finger. While holding down the G/E♭ double stop with the ring finger, play the A and A♭ notes with the index finger and then place the middle finger on the D note on string 3, at the same time keeping the ring finger on the G note on string 2. After playing the D/A♭ notes with the same fingering, move the index and middle fingers down one fret to D♭/G while the ring finger continues to maintain the G as a pedal tone.

Fig. 1

Melody (1st 32 meas.)

* played slightly ahead of the beat

Guitar Notation Legend

Guitar Music can be notated three different ways: on a *musical staff*, in *tablature*, and in *rhythm slashes*.

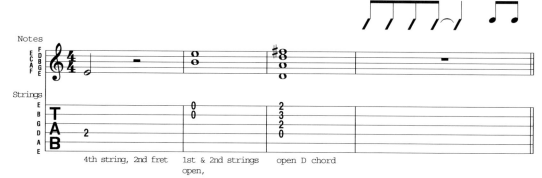

RHYTHM SLASHES are written above the staff. Strum chords in the rhythm indicated. Use the chord diagrams found at the top of the first page of the transcription for the appropriate chord voicings. Round noteheads indicate single notes.

THE MUSICAL STAFF shows pitches and rhythms and is divided by bar lines into measures. Pitches are named after the first seven letters of the alphabet.

TABLATURE graphically represents

4th string, 2nd fret open, 1st & 2nd strings open, open D chord

HALF-STEP BEND: Strike the note and bend up 1/2 step.

WHOLE-STEP BEND: Strike the note and bend up one step.

GRACE NOTE BEND: Strike the note and bend up as indicated. The first note does not

SLIGHT (MICROTONE) BEND: Strike the note and bend up 1/4 step.

BEND AND RELEASE: Strike the note and bend up as indicated, then release back to the original note.

PRE-BEND: Bend the note as indicated, then strike it.

VIBRATO: The string is vibrated by rapidly bending and releasing the note with the fretting hand.

WIDE VIBRATO: The pitch is varied to a greater degree by vibrating with the fretting hand.

HAMMER-ON: Strike the first (lower) note with one finger, then sound the higher note (on the same string) with another finger by fretting it without

PULL-OFF: Place both fingers on the notes to be sounded. Strike the first note and without picking, pull the finger off to sound the second

LEGATO SLIDE: Strike the first note and then slide the same fret-hand finger up or down to the second note. The second note is not

SHIFT SLIDE: Same as legato slide, except the second note is struck.

TRILL: Very rapidly alternate between the notes indicated by continuously hammering on and

TAPPING: Hammer ("tap") the fret indicated with the pick-hand index or middle finger and pull off to the note fretted by the fret hand.

NATURAL HARMONIC: Strike the note while the fret-hand lightly touches the string directly over the fret

PINCH HARMONIC: The note is fretted normally and a harmonic is produced by adding the edge of the thumb or the tip of the index finger of the pick

PICK SCRAPE: The edge of the pick is rubbed down (or up) the string, producing a scratchy sound.

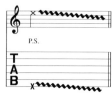

MUFFLED STRINGS: A percussive sound is produced by laying the fret hand across the string(s) without depressing, and striking them with the pick hand.

PALM MUTING: The note is partially muted by the pick hand lightly touching the string(s) just before

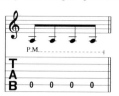

RAKE: Drag the pick across the strings indicated with a single motion.

TREMOLO PICKING: The note is picked as rapidly and continuously as possible.

VIBRATO BAR DIVE AND RETURN: The pitch of the note or chord is dropped a specified number of steps (in rhythm) then returned to the original

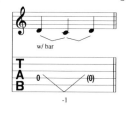

VIBRATO BAR SCOOP: Depress the bar just before striking the note, then quickly release the bar.

VIBRATO BAR DIP: Strike the note and then immediately drop a specified number of steps, then release back to the original pitch.